SOME THINGS
REMEMBERED

Photo by Katherine L. Krieghbaum, Jr.

SOME THINGS REMEMBERED

Hillier Krieghbaum
Kay Krieghbaum
Katherine L. Krieghbaum, Jr.

HARBOR HILL BOOKS

Harrison, New York

1982

Library of Congress Cataloging in Publication Data

Krieghbaum, Hillier.
  Some things remembered.

  1. Krieghbaum, Kay, 1916–1959.
  2. Krieghbaum, Kay L. (Katherine Lancaster), 1946–1969. 3. Krieghbaum, Hillier. 4. United States—Biography. I. Krieghbaum, Kay, 1916–1959. II. Krieghbaum, Katherine L. (Katherine Lancaster), 1946–1969. III. Title.
  CT275.K873K74   973'.09'92 [B]   81-20097
  ISBN 0-916346-44-7   AACR2

Copyright © 1982 by Hillier Krieghbaum
All rights reserved.

No part of this book may be used or reproduced in any manner whatsoever without permission except in the case of brief quotations embodied in critical articles and reviews.

Edited by Hugh Rawson

Designed by Judith Woracek Mullen

FIRST EDITION

Printed in the United States of America

For information, address
Harbor Hill Books, P.O. Box 407, Harrison, N.Y. 10528

CONTENTS

Part One
HILLIER KRIEGHBAUM

1. Background for a Family Portrait   3

Part Two
KAY KRIEGHBAUM

2. Country Living: Growing-up Years   39

3. City and Suburban Years   68

Part Three
KATHERINE L. KRIEGHBAUM, JR.

4. From Kay-K's Notebook   141

5. People and Places: A Photographic Album   146

I've done the best I could with what I've had,
    Few things that could not be improved upon.
I cannot claim I am satisfied
    But this for the defense I swear: I tried.

God knows, I never yet have claimed to be satisfied.
    I grant that many tasks are treason to the heart
That cries upon perfection, but I think
    Perfection is for angels, not for men.

Kay Krieghbaum

It's my way . . .
I love the way I want.
I learn the way I want.
I worship the way I want.
I speak of what I want the way I want.
I am what I have made myself.
I am what I have experienced.
Why don't I know myself?
Because . . .
    It's *my* way.

Kay L. Krieghbaum, Jr.

Part One

HILLIER KRIEGHBAUM

1. Background for a Family Portrait

Each individual has a chance to leave a record that contributes to the mainstream of human existence. This is immortality, of a sort. Some have a long run and others only a strictly limited time. Some leave behind only memories in the minds of friends and relatives. Others furnish more tangible things such as writings, paintings, and other material works.

Since I feel it is imperative that ideas be shared, I have tried to do just that with this book of reminiscences and pictures by my wife and daughter. Both died suddenly, a decade apart, before they had an opportunity to prepare their works for publication. So I am sharing these samplings of their philosophies of life and nature that I discovered after they died.

Obviously, in this context, I am no objective critic. But I am convinced that both were talented and on the verge of attaining at least modest successes with their writing and photography. This book attempts to disseminate their contributions which otherwise might have remained in files and been forgotten. Amazing to me has been the great similarity of reactions of mother and daughter despite the generational difference.

My wife, Katherine Lancaster Krieghbaum, was born in Brooklyn, New York, on November 18, 1916. She was graduated from Smith College in 1938, worked in Washington on the *Times-Herald* and, during World War II, for the War Shipping Administration and War Production Board. There I met her and we were married June 6, 1945. We spent a year in Eugene, Oregon, while I taught at the University of Oregon, then we moved to Mamaroneck, New York, in 1947. She died of a brain tumor on March 27, 1959.

For some years before her death, Kay kept a private folder of her writings and the following texts are from it. Once, when we were in Oregon, Kay left a manuscript on which she had been working beside the typewriter, where I found it after she had gone to bed. I could not resist looking over her pages and the next morning made a comment on a possible revision. She explained with both fervor and validity her rights to privacy. After that, I never read any of her writings without her permission. Thus, I never saw most of these articles until after she had died.

Katherine L. Krieghbaum, Jr., or "Kay-K" as we called our daughter, was born in Washington, D.C., on April 1, 1946, and went to elementary schools in Mamaroneck. After her mother's death, she attended the Northampton School for Girls and Northwestern University, from which she was graduated with a major in history in the Class of 1968. A month's stay in Japan during 1960 while I was participating in two science writing conferences kindled an interest in Oriental philosophy and arts—areas in which she took elective courses at Northwestern.

A photography course in the Medill School of Journalism at Northwestern taught her the techniques for expressing her ideas in this medium. After her graduation, she attended the New York Institute of Photography and sharpened her competence. She was killed by a hit-and-run driver early in the morning of August 8, 1969, near Bloody Pond Road in the summer resort area of Lake George, New York.

When I offered her a graduation present of a European trip, Kay-K asked, "Daddy, may I use the money for a really good camera and equipment?" I agreed. Thus she had the tools of her trade. She shot many of the photographs in this volume during the first seven months of 1969.

❖ ❖ ❖

It was the last week of January, 1945, when I first met my future wife on a blind date at the University Club in Washington, D.C. I was with the Navy on duty in a barrack-like office on Constitution Avenue — a "tempo" left over from an earlier World War. Another Navy officer, a *Time* correspondent, and I shared an apartment overlooking Rock Creek Park near the Connecticut Avenue Bridge. We worked on matters military during the daytime and partied many of the nights. In that fourth year of fighting, regardless of what dangers were faced (and I faced none), many Washingtonians lived by the philosophy that there might be no tomorrow and socialized "full speed ahead."

To say that it was "love at first sight" would be melodramatic but I did find Kay attractive, intelligent, and interesting company. I asked her for another date — and then another. A letter that turned up in my mother's papers when I examined them after her death in 1956 reminded me that when I had first written about meeting Kay, I had added that I hoped to marry her. That probably was within a month of our University Club introduction.

Kay was working as an economist with the War Production Board. (She had an honors degree in economics from Smith College—along with a Phi Beta Kappa key.) Her work seemed far more exciting than mine. I codified statistics on all Navy airplane crashes, including "secret" reports. We had a "confidential trashman" who came around late each afternoon to collect classified materials that we had discarded. Kay, by contrast, confided one time about how she and her woman superior had met with their British opposites and allocated the entire Allied supply of nylon for military and civilian use. Jokingly, she added, "And we sat there barelegged when we did it."

Another of Kay's stories of that period concerned a bureaucratic misadventure about "hemp" in China. The British came storming into her War Production Board office one day, accusing the Americans of holding out on some strategic supply of Chinese hemp. As evidence, they cited a cablegram in which the short-supply hemp was mentioned. Upon checking, Kay was assured by knowledgeable sources, "There is no hemp in China." The suspicious British were unconvinced, so Kay telephoned the message center of the Department of State and, after some argument, got the cablegram re-decoded. A typographical error had crept in; the word should have been "hump." The decoder, questioned at home, said that when she looked up "hump" in the dictionary, she thought "hemp" made more sense, so she substituted it. Definitely, however, there was a "hump" in China and Allied airplanes were flying over it daily. Thus, the British were convinced that China and the United States were not hoarding a secret stockpile of hemp.

When President Franklin D. Roosevelt died in April, I called Kay to learn if she had heard the news. She had. News of monumental events, as communication researchers were to document later when President John F. Kennedy died, travels initially by word of mouth. And I could also have told them that the person who passes along the news generally does it to those who are closest to him or her.

Kay and I decided to be "engaged" but we felt there was no rush to get married. Then I got a tentative assignment to go to Europe, either England or France, to join the journalism faculty that was being set up to teach soldiers and sailors in Europe after the war there came to a close. It was expected that thousands of servicemen would be backed up in Europe, simply because not enough ships were available to bring them home or to the Pacific. Dean Kenneth E. Olson, of Northwestern Univerity, explained that the job carried a simulated rank of colonel or lieutenant-colonel in the U.S. Army. I said that I was a "real" lieutenant in the Naval Reserve and that I would much prefer that rank althought it was lower than the simulated one. He replied that he thought this would cause no problem. When I told Kay, we decided to get married and called our respective mothers, mine in South Bend, Indiana, and hers in Worcester, Massachusetts. Wartime train travel was difficult but our parents arrived so that we could be married on June 6, 1945: "D-Day plus 365" as we called it on our anniversaries.

Since the District of Columbia required a waiting period, the ceremony took place at a federal installation in nearby Maryland. With a touch of irony, our wedding announcements told that the event had taken place at the Fort Lincoln Cemetery. That caused quite a few inquiries from friends and relatives.

Since I had already taken some leave during the previous year, my request for leave to go on a honeymoon included a statement that I intended to be married during the period. Approval came back endorsed "by direction" for Fleet Admiral Ernest J. King, Chief of Naval Operations. I occasionally teased Kay that once the chief Navy officer had approved our marriage, I never had a chance to change my mind. Not that I wanted to!

We left for a honeymoon, first to Virginia Beach, near the Norfolk Naval Air Station, where I had been stationed for more than a year and which I wanted to show to Kay. The first morning at Virginia Beach, the sun was overcast. Kay and I went to the beach in our swim suits and, before we realized, several hours had passed. That night we spent considerable time smearing lotions on each other. Not, I guarantee, a recommended way to spend part of a honeymoon. The rest of the time, we spent in Worcester, where I met her relatives, and at Martha's Vineyard.

When we got back to Washington, I found that the European assignment had fallen through. I never did discover whether the Army didn't want a "real" lieutenant on the faculty, or what. At least, Kay and I were together in a third floor walk-up apartment near Washington Cathedral instead of three thousand miles apart.

I was separated from the Navy in early October and Kay and I went to Bermuda with an old friend, a former newspaperman, and his wife for part of our terminal leaves. We encountered a photographer for the soon-to-be-launched *Holiday* magazine and every time he took a picture that included Kay, all the rest of us would dig a slight depression in the sand so her pregnancy would not be visible to the magazine's future readers. Mores in 1945 were somewhat different than today.

Our friends, the Pinkertons, shared a pixy sense of humor, which created a mystery for the two Krieghbaums. Our guest-house hostess, who originally had been most friendly in her rather formal British way, suddenly turned rather cool. We couldn't figure out why. Much later, the Pinkertons confessed that they had told the cottage manager we had just been married and were on our honeymoon. That news was four months out of date—and so was Kay's figure.

We agreed that if we had a boy, Kay would pick the name, and if we had a girl, I would. I decided I wanted a "Jr." and even called the Library of Congress to make sure that women could use "Jr." as well as men. The term could apply to either sex I was told.

Our pediatrician, who had been a neighbor of mine at the Rock Creek Park apartment, predicted the baby should arrive the end of March or early April. Kay insisted that she wanted to insure her child was not born on April Fool's Day. None of that type of kidding for her offspring! Her plans didn't work out.

On Sunday, March 31, the doctor and his wife were among our dinner guests. The turkey was so large that we had to take it out of the oven to baste it. Since Kay was extremely pregnant, I lifted the fowl out of the oven, placed it on the floor, and went to work with a syringe.

Labor pains started around 1 a.m. or 2 a.m. and I, trying to be practical, started timing them. The tempo increased slowly and about 7 o'clock, I called the doctor at home. His wife, realizing it was April Fool's Day, demanded, "Are you playing a trick on us?" I said, "No," and offered to take the phone into our bedroom so that the physician could check the time between pains. Within an hour, he arrived with his car. (We didn't have one.) The two of us helped Kay down to the second floor landing, and then, after a pause, into the auto. At the hospital, we reversed the process until an aide arrived with a wheelchair. I stayed around trying to be helpful—or, at least, to look that way—until Kay told our doctor friend to send me to the Veterans' Administration where I was working as a public information specialist. I made her nervous, she said. I looked so distressed when she had a pain.

That morning, General Paul Hawley, VA Chief Medical Officer, was to be interviewed by a reporter and I was supposed to join the group as part of my job. I looked at my watch. I thought they would never stop talking. Finally they did and I rushed back to my office. Yes, a message was on the middle of my desk. Our daughter had been born at about 11:30 a.m. I took a long lunch break that day.

I saw Kay-K in the nursery before Kay had first nursed her. So I was a sort of reporter to my own wife. I reported that Kay-K was "defective" because she had a tuft of blonde hair amid the brown in the middle of her forehead. My choice of words nearly headed us into the divorce court right then. (As a teen-ager, Kay-K still had this natural streak—which some of her contemporaries spent near fortunes to attain by means of bleaches.)

I gave Kay a sterling silver charm in the form of a baby carriage for her already-long bracelet. Eventually it included such momentoes as a miniature U.S. Capitol, an airplane (for our trip to Oregon), and a cable car (in memory of a visit to San Francisco).

Our top-floor apartment was hot that summer with no air-conditioner to be purchased; wartime shortages were not yet over. Kay and Kay-K, however, seemed to thrive. My work at the Veterans' Adminstration grew less and less attractive as bureaucracy returned more and more to its pre-war patterns. Kay had predicted that I would stand a government job for not more than six months. She was slightly off target; I left in a little less than a year. My former Kansas State College boss, who was supposed to become dean of the University of Oregon journalism school in 1947, got me an offer to teach at Eugene, Oregon. I accepted. I was to report in September at the opening of the 1946-47 school year. Kay hurried around to get such supplies as extra diapers and, praise be, the last electric refrigerator at Woodward and Lothrop department store until postwar production resumed. The freight bill was fantastic but we had been assured that there probably was not an unsold refrigerator in the whole state of Oregon.

A group of our Washington friends gave us a send-off at the airport. One of Kay's former fellow workers at the War Shipping Administration gave us the Portland address of his mother-in-law—just in case. We felt much like pioneers following the Lewis and Clark trail of nearly one hundred and fifty years earlier. As it turned out, that thought was not too much fantasy despite the twentieth century setting. Our transcontinental flight required a stop at Chicago but our departure from the airport was delayed. Accomodations for feeding babies had been omitted from the architect's blueprints. So we had to feed Kay-K in a crowded waiting room and without even the most elementary facilities for heating baby-bottles. To keep our daughter from screaming at the top of her lungs from changing air pressures, we doped her with soothing syrup that our pediatrician had provided. Kay and I read and re-read the label to learn how much we could administer without risking a lethal dosage.

Arriving at the airport in Portland, Kay-K was cooing gleefully while her parents were exhausted. We called Mrs. Watkins about the offer of hospitality and she graciously invited us to spend a day with her. Her daughter had alerted her by telegram while we were flying across the continent. She even helped us locate a practical nurse to watch our five-month-old while we caught up on sleep and got our diaper supply ready for future use.

In Eugene, we found that our little home in the West had only a wood-burning stove and no central heating system. One of my first tasks was to buy wood; then I had to stack some in a hall closet near the stove and pile the rest in a shed near the house. For the entire ten months we were in Oregon, I battled that stove but, no matter what procedure, I seldom could set a fire at night that would leave any smouldering embers when I crawled out of a warm bed in the morning. Even setting an alarm clock for dawn didn't help.

An open fireplace in the living room might have helped the heating but our active youngster was intent in converting it into a playpen regardless of how many ashes remained from a previous night's fire. We finally built a barrier that would withstand her sturdy attacks—but the result was that we barely could get it down for our own use of the fireplace.

A hasty check for other possible quarters revealed not a chance of moving. The GI rush to college in that early postwar year had produced an equivalent of the California gold rush of 1849. Only this near stampede was for nuggets of knowledge, not gold. Landholders profited by renting space for campers on their properties. A single lot could have as many as four homes crowded together on it.

Oregon journalism students were an intriguing group and we saw a lot of them. They had travelled much of the world in the armed services and some had undergone the traumatically maturing experience of seeing their comrades suffer and die in battle. One air veteran had been written up in a *New Yorker* magazine profile as "Young Man Behind Plexiglass." Kay and I spent many fascinating evenings hearing about their experiences, their future plans, and the world they hoped to make. All of us enjoyed talking about journalism.

Like most parents with only one child, we had our nervous doubts about the conduct of our offspring but fortunately we had a competent and reassuring doctor. There was the time when Kay-K, playing on the lawn, began a diet of grubs. What to do? A hurried and harried phone call reached our physician. He heard the story and commented, "Don't worry. The grubs probably have some sort of antibiotic."

During one office visit, Kay inquired about the time when Kay-K should say that dramatic first word. The baby books mostly cited a time that had already passed. The MD asked how much we translated of the babble that came from our child. Then he explained, "Why should she learn to talk? You are responding to her demands without formal language." We both became less responsive and Kay-K fast became a conversationalist in English, not babble-talk.

Trying to adjust our somewhat sybaritic concepts of metropolitan living to the jam-packed, boom-town conditions of Eugene never was completely resolved. Kay found some domestic help from a migrant worker's wife who gave up her factory job at fifty cents an hour for the easier work of housecleaning and baby-sitting. As Christmas approached, we agreed that we had jumped too rapidly, and without enough preparation, when we left Washington. A real blow came when the dean-designate put a note on his holiday card that he was staying in Washington and wasn't coming to Oregon, after all.

From then on, I began a campaign for another job. The new one, I hoped, would be in a metropolitan center. A trip to San Francisco provided a visit to one of my favorite cities but no attractive job possibility. So Kay would not feel cheated out of one of the few pleasures of our Western experience, I baby-sat for one long weekend while she saw San Francisco. She was even more excited by the city and its people than I was. "When I die, I don't want to go to heaven," she said. "I just want to go to San Francisco."

Before we left Eugene, Kay posed with the baby carriage in front of a sculptured tribute to the Pioneer Woman. Kay had a hand on her hip and was looking up in dismay, not admiration, at what the earlier generation of women must have put up with. Possibly, our living in Eastern seaboard metropolitan areas had disqualified us for the postwar college boom town. (Years later, when I returned to Eugene to lecture on my field of science writing, I found that life could be quite comfortable indeed. There was ample housing. It was too bad that Kay could not have been alive to have joined me.)

Some Washington friends told us about a summer sublet near Georgetown University in Washington. We had decided to establish a base in that metropolis but before we flew East, I began negotiating for a position as information specialist with the United Nations World Health Organization, which was then being established with an office in New York City.

The trip back to Washington from Oregon, like the flight out, had its delays and we "doped" our daughter in the Portland airport much as we had on the way out. Since the airplane wasn't crowded, we built a nest of pillows on two seats for Kay-K to stretch out on. One vivid recollection is the sight of Great Salt Lake as we flew over it. The moon was up and the salty water reflected like a huge jewel in the darkness. And our daughter was sleeping quietly.

When we arrived at the D.C. sublet we discovered more than we had bargained for. There was Steuben glassware, obviously wedding presents to the owner's bride, and cockroaches in the kitchen. Kay speculated, "I wonder if the hostess ever visited her own kitchen." We arranged to keep a limited supply of silver and dishes in the refrigerator, which fortunately was roach-proof.

We decided to have a cocktail party for our Washington friends, after making sure that we could bug-proof the kitchen for at least a few hours. The morning of the party, Kay-K started screaming in agony and we discovered that one of her teeth was pushing against an unbreakable gum. Our MD friend, who was to be a party guest, came to the rescue and lanced our daughter's stubborn gum. And just as we were considering calling off the party, Kay-K quieted down and the nurse we had hired to look after her did a superb job of keeping her both cheerful and quiet.

The WHO job came through and I started working in New York City while Kay and Kay-K stayed in Georgetown. It was an intriguing assignment in the public health field, my task being to place articles to promote the United Nations agency. When a cholera epidemic broke out in Egypt that summer, the WHO sent vaccine in by air. I put out releases announcing shipments to stall the spread of the epidemic but the only story that got major display told how a racehorse had been "bumped" from one flight so that the medicines could be flown. My New York regional superior felt I should exploit

WHO in the same manner as his family's chain of Long Island theaters. Our differences eventually led to my leaving the agency but not until I had gone to Geneva, Switzerland, to help publicize a session of the interim commission, which comprised health ministers or diplomatic representatives from eighteen countries.

Kay and I found that a couple with an eighteen-month-old youngster were not considered the most desired tenants for apartments and sublets. The signs said "No pets" but, to be truthful, most of them could well have displayed "No children," too. We began looking for a house to buy in Westchester and found one in Mamaroneck. We thought it would be a good base for further house-hunting, but it turned out to be our permanent home. The last weekend I was in the country before I left for Geneva, Kay came up and, as they say, we "did the town" for a couple of days — shows, dinners, and a bit of sightseeing.

Before I went to the airport, I wrote a short note to Kay and mailed it to our Washington address. "Darling," it read, "Just a line to let you know I love you very much. Thanks for everything. This will come after I have left for Europe." I had flown a lot, including sixty hours logged in my Navy records as my superior took me along for company while he fulfilled his monthly requirement for extra flight pay. However, I have never learned to feel completely sure of returning from any long flight. My note to Kay must have touched her because years later she showed it to me. Some of the ink had been smeared by a couple of tears. I guess we were both sentimentalists.

Kay, Kay-K, and Lucille, a nurse, came to our new home in Mamaroneck. They settled in with movers, carpenters, and roofers while I was in Geneva. Although I had little spare time to sightsee in Geneva, I did watch the magnificent Jet d'Eau fountain play at Lake Leman with Mount Blanc in the distant background. A magnificent sight on a clear day! I wrote to Kay about the experience. When that letter arrived, Kay was having trouble with the sewage system and in no mood for descriptions of scenic sights in foreign lands. She told me when I returned that only Lucille's strongest arguments had prevented her from sending me a cable — collect, no doubt — saying:

"Forget Lake Leman. Come home and swim in cellar sewage."

The workmen building book shelves and measuring for storm windows provided much entertainment for Kay-K. One day she watched a carpenter outside the living room window and struggled to draw a low coffee table over to the window for a better look. As she got there, the workman climbed down and Kay-K muttered an exclamation that both her mother and visiting grandmother said sounded like a very juvenile "damn." And where had she learned that word at eighteen months?

Lots of work had to be done around the house to adapt it to our special needs. Kay redesigned the kitchen. She had expertly drawn the plans—to the last measurement—and I supplied a sturdy back and muscle-power to saw and nail in new cupboards and to move some of the permanent plantings in the garden. Then there was the job of installing a "jungle gym" for our preschool activist. Kay-K adapted to the swings and ladders as if she were a monkey and became so expert at hanging by her feet from bars that her Grandmother Lancaster nearly collapsed when she saw her performing one day. It was a busy fall and winter, especially since I was working full time.

By Christmas of 1947, it seemed certain that my career at WHO was going to be shortlived and I arranged to teach journalism courses at New York University during the spring semester. Students in those immediate postwar years were, as they had been at Oregon, an exciting group and there were so many of them that the University scheduled some classes in the suburbs because space was unavailable in regular campus buildings. One class I had that spring was held in the afternoon at the White Plains High School and I had gotten the assignment because it was in a neighboring town.

Never fond of housekeeping, Kay devoted herself more and more to her garden. At the same time, she instilled a lasting love of nature in her daughter. (Possibly that accounts, in part, for the numerous nature shots in our daughter's photographs included in this book.) Kay took a special interest in herbs. She grew a wide variety and dried them for her own cooking and for Christmas presents to close friends and relatives.

To build a special wild flower garden along the northern side of our house, Kay and I excavated the poor soil next to our basement and replaced it with peat moss and other enrichments. Kay did the plans and I supplied the back-power for digging out the earth and wheel-barrowing it down to fill in an eroding river bank at the bottom of River Street. We must have done a good job because even now, nearly a quarter century later, each spring has its jack-in-the-pulpits, trilliums, and wild yellow lilies—despite my lack of care.

One irony arose from the herb gardens she planted. She especially wanted to grow chervil and tried it in several plots that she thought were favorable. It grew, but with mixed results. Then, the summer after she died, a large stand of chervil appeared, without much attention from me, under our raspberry bushes, and at least a bit of chervil grew from self-sown seeds in the backyard for years.

Another release for Kay during those early years in Mamaroneck was playing a minor role in politics. She was attracted to Henry Wallace's presidential effort in 1948. Years later, during questioning for a Naval Reserve "secret" clearance, I was asked if I had ever voted for a candidate other than one of the two major parties. I responded, "Yes, for Henry Wallace in 1948." I did get my clearance orders but only after some months delay. We both followed Adlai Stevenson's campaigns with enthusiasm and Kay was elected a precinct committeewoman shortly before she died. However, she was an individualist always and never was entirely comfortable with organized groups of any sort. While she had a full-blown social conscience, she also remained a private person when she herself was concerned.

Kay had wanted to add a cat to our household after we got our residence in somewhat normal order. I was reluctant because I never had pets when I was a boy and wondered if I really wanted an animal in the house. Later, I learned that Kay had told one of her friends that having a cat as a pet was considered the "only major difference" between us. Eventually, Kay (with some help from Kay-K) won and we went over to the Westchester Humane Society late one afternoon to pick not one, but two, small cats. Kay chose the names—"Beer" and "Skittles"—to demonstrate that now everything was all right, at least in the way of pets. Skittles, it turned out, was unwell and died some months later. Beer, a fluffy black and white animal with at least one ancestor that was a Persian, survived into his second decade and outlived my wife. With Kay directing, I built a small swinging entry in our back door so that the cats could come and go as they pleased. This provided our animals with freedom but once or twice a tomcat used it to invade our kitchen and living room, and a real donnybrook ensued to chase the marauder out.

Beer had his circle of neighborhood friends and a cat from next door played with him as if the two were kittens instead of gentlemen in sedate middle age. Kay planted catnip among her herbs. That provided fresh and dried herbs for Beer and his friend but also once led to a garden full of cat hairs when two toms contested for at least a half hour over their territorial rights. We almost had to get a rake to clear the debris away after the fight ended.

Beer frequently enjoyed supervising Kay (and sometimes Kay-K) when garden work had to be done. Once, Kay was carefully digging small holes for herb cuttings. So the plants could root better, she put water into each hole. Beer, always a fastidious cat who even covered up spots where his carefree feline neighbor had been remiss in completing his toilet, promptly followed Kay and began filling with dirt each hole awaiting a cutting. Eventually, Kay had to put him in the house so that she could finish her job without interference.

Sunday mornings Kay and I tried sleeping late and we trained our active youngster to play in her bed until we got up. One morning there was an agonized cry from Kay-K's room and I dashed out to see what was wrong. Our daughter was as puzzled as I was but Beer was parading triumphantly. Under Kay-K's bed was a terrified baby rabbit that he had brought in as proof of his prowess as a mighty hunter. Although we could not find any bruises, the baby rabbit was dead by the time I put it out in the yard. Apparently it had died of fright, just after its final, all-too-human wail.

Another episode was not so lethal although it resulted in a bloody mess in the kitchen. A bewildered pheasant flew directly into the window pane facing the gardens. We recovered him on the floor, bleeding like a chicken with its head chopped off. Annoyed by the blood spurting all over the floor, I grabbed the bird, opened the back door, and threw it as far away as I could. The bird lay on the ground for a few seconds and then flew away. For part of that day, I searched our yard and those of our neighbors trying to find a dead pheasant. It was in vain.

Some years after we had settled into our River Street residence, we heard of new neighbors, the Vollenweiders, arriving. Kay learned that Al Vollenweider had been graduated from Wisconsin, which was my alma mater, too. So, from that common bond, we became good friends. The Vollenweiders helped us mix and pour the concrete for a solid base for our washing machine, and Kay and I helped them plant small trees and shrubs. Flossie Vollenweider still recalls the time that she saw us coming down the hill to their house and then turned around suddenly. We had seen them digging a hole for a new tree and had gone back for our tools so that we could help.

Raising a youngster can, as all parents find out, be complicated. For instance, our next door neighbors had a daughter approximately eighteen months older than our Kay-K. The two played together much of the time. And, as usually happens with preschool children, the slightly older one wanted—and generally got—her way. If not, a tussle might result. So Kay tried to explain that, if Suzie hit her, it was all right for Kay-K to hit back. A couple of days later, Suzie went home screaming. Kay asked what had happened and Kay-K replied, "I hit her back first."

One of my playful wisecracks came home to haunt me when I was about to turn fifty. I jokingly explained to Kay-K that I was entering my second half-century. I thought it was a good gag. Imagine my surprise a couple of days later to hear my daughter skipping up and down the street, chanting at the top of her voice, "My Daddy is entering his second half-century; my Daddy is entering his second half-century." Also, I found out that my comment had been my daughter's contribution for "Show and Tell" at school.

Kay-K joined the Girl Scouts and, when she became eligible, she went off to summer camp. It was her first long separation from her parents and we were delighted when we got an enthusiastic post card telling about her pets (a lizard and frog, I believe) and including a dozen "X's" for kisses for each of us. A couple of days later she wrote that her teeth braces had broken when she bit into a piece of candy and that she was so sorry because she hadn't meant to break them. As Kay noted in her journal, it probably was the toughest letter that our twelve-year-old had had to write up to that time. When we went to pick her up at camp, we found she had won "Best Camper" award. Even more rewarding to Kay and me was the unsolicited compliment from her counselor that she had been a real pleasure, with the enthusiasms of her age unspoiled by the sophistication of some of her contemporaries who used lipstick and other talismans of maturing too fast too young.

Among the games that we played while travelling by automobile was one of trying to be the first to spot a gopher as we sped along the expressways to see distant friends. It was a variation of the generations-old sport of counting white horses or some other infrequently-seen animal. Another variation that we developed was to spot the alphabet on license plates in proper sequence with the winner being the one who first found the final "Z."

One Christmas, Kay decided to give me what I said I wanted: the wartime edition of Franklin D. Roosevelt's public papers for 1937-1940. I had managed to purchase the first five and the last four volumes of FDR's papers because I wanted to research transcripts of his press conferences as part of my study of Washington news gathering. She contacted many of the Third Avenue book shops that specialized in out-of-print books. However, the wartime edition was small and copies were hard to locate. Christmas approached without any luck. Among my presents that year was a hand-written scroll telling of her vain search and promising to keep on looking. In the spring, she presented me with the missing books. Late but no less appreciated.

When President Eisenhower ordered U.S. Marines into Lebanon in 1958, the news was especially grim for a Naval Reservist such as I was. Kay, Kay-K, and I set aside a holiday for a safari to the Catskill Game Farm, where we could enjoy the animals and build memories that would be worth looking back on—just in case an aging reservist was called up for duty. Nothing like active duty occurred but it was an especially nice trip anyway.

During the summer of that same year, the state was hurrying to complete the New England Thruway behind our house, so that Governor Averell Harriman could claim it as a political plus in his campaign that fall against Nelson Rockefeller. The workmen had to clear out a woods across the river from our street for the roadway. Kay and our neighbor Flossie lamented the loss of homes for wild animals and birds as the whining buzz saws cut into the trunks of the trees that they had learned to love. Their only consolation was the replanting in their own yards of some flowers and young trees that were scheduled for destruction so that tons of concrete roadway could replace them.

At the end of January, 1959, Kay complained of headaches and we started going to doctors. First, one suspected that it might be nicotine poisoning from her heavy cigarette smoking. She made a noble and successful effort to break a years-old habit, putting aside in a jar the money she would have spent for cigarettes, meaning to treat herself to something special later on when she was well. The pains continued. So she had her eyes checked but nothing serious was wrong with them. Eventually, a neurologist was recommended and he suspected a brain tumor. Late in March, he proposed a brain scan and Kay was hospitalized. The results showed a brain tumor and it was decided that she should undergo exploratory surgery.

The afternoon before she was to have the operation, I went into the city to New York University to take care of a few necessary jobs and then up to the hospital to visit Kay. On the subway ride, I thought to myself, "I'm sitting down but if I give my seat to that elderly woman over there, will Kay have a better chance to recover?" The idea was crazy but eventually I offered the seat to the woman. Was this some sort of primeval perception of what might be—or just a weird twisting of a mind under emotional pressure? At the hospital, I tried to reassure Kay and we talked about what we would do in the future.

The next day I worked around the house to prepare it for her mother's arrival that afternoon. I arranged for a neighbor to take Kay-K over to pick up her Grandmother Lancaster at the station and then I went to the hospital. While I was waiting to go to Kay's room, I heard a series of emergency calls over the loudspeaker system. The idea occurred to me that it might be Kay's room. The impression grew stronger when I was told to wait before going to Kay's floor. Time passed. Finally, a doctor told me that she was in a crisis and was unconscious. He insisted that I could be of no help in the hospital and so, reluctantly, I went home. Just after arriving there, I got a telephone call from the hospital saying that Kay was dead. After I told Mrs. Lancaster and my daughter, Kay-K ran upstairs to be alone and closed the door to her room. Her grandmother and I stayed downstairs to talk and to plan.

On one of the rare times when Kay and I had talked about

funerals and burials, she said that she violently disapproved of open coffins and formal church services. So at the funeral, the coffin was closed and the service, arranged with a sympathetic local Methodist minister, consisted of some of Kay's favorite readings, quite a few from *The Prophet* by Kahil Gibran.

Kay-K's thirteenth birthday was two days after her mother's funeral. I was determined that her entry into the teens would not go unnoted, so Kay-K, her grandmother, and I went to a Connecticut steak house where we undoubtedly would have gone if her mother had been around and well. (There is a touch of irony about the choice: On one of Kay's birthdays the three of us had gone to the same place and I, kiddingly, had asked if she wanted the waiters to sing, "Happy Birthday," as they often did. She responded, "You do that and I'll see you in the divorce court." She wasn't entirely joking, either.)

Years later, one of our friends told me that Mrs. Lancaster had confided to her that she had had a hard time understanding her granddaughter's reactions: Some months after Kay's death, Kay-K had come into the kitchen one morning and announced that she had been thinking about her mother's death and decided that she was going to live her own life without more grieving.

After Kay's death, we did our best to rebuild our family structure. Mrs. Lancaster, who had retired from her department store job in Worcester, Massachusetts, only a few months before her daughter became sick, agreed to come to Mamaroneck to help out. Over the next few months, we worked out a plan so that Kay-K would continue in the eighth grade in the fall of 1959; her grandmother would keep her apartment in Worcester but spend most of her time with us. With new ground rules demanded, Kay-K did what I called, "testing in strength." Her mother was gone; her grandmother and I had not been around as much previously as now. So, like any intelligent youngster, she wanted new freedoms in a different situation. Trying to be an understanding single parent, I was aware that the rules had to be re-oriented but it was not done without some minor traumas for all of us. I thought it would be unfair for Mrs. Lancaster to abandon entirely her Worcester apartment where she had lived for nearly a third of a century and began looking at girls' boarding schools. The one I picked was the academic descendant of one that "Grandma" Lancaster had attended: The Northampton School for Girls. The headmistress had been a young first-year instructor in those days so Kay-K was well welcomed as representing the third generation.

Now fourteen years old, my daughter wasn't completely sold on leaving home; most teen-agers probably have the same reaction about that initial jump out of the family nest. I had promised her that she and I would tour the Western National Parks and bought a new second-hand car to make the trip. Then I was offered a chance to visit Japan to participate in two science writing seminars. When I replied that I would not go without my daughter, the offer seemed to disappear. A day or two after July 4, however, I got a call from San Francisco, summarized as, "It's all set."

"What's all set?" I asked.

"You and your daughter will leave for Japan on July 19."

The explanation was that the two of us would fly tourist class with the money that had been budgeted for my going alone, first class. I said, "Call me back over the weekend, after we've talked it over." My most persuasive presentation of things we could do and sights we would see was only partly effective, but Kay-K started to become enthusiastic when the parents of her best Mamaroneck friend told of acquaintances who now lived in Tokyo and loved it. Kay-K and I had to rush to get the required medical shots for our vaccination certificates. (The final one, for cholera, actually was done in Japan with a certifying stamp, about the size of a postal card.)

The Japanese were delightful hosts. We were there under the auspices of the Asia Foundation, San Francisco, for travel and the Japan Newspaper Publishers and Editors Association (JNPEA) for the time in their country. While I was participating in two three-day science writing seminars, one in Tokyo and one in Osaka, a young JNPEA representative took Kay-K on special visits that would interest a teenager. I had to learn to speak "translation-ese" (in which one speaks for a minute or two and then stops for the translation). Our work out of the way, another JNPEA staff member from the International section was assigned to escort us to many of Japan's show spots.

There was Kyushu, the southernmost isle, where we stayed in a Japanese inn and I was nearly scalded in a hot, spring-fed bath. Also the shrine at Miyajima, where Kay-K took a photograph of the brilliant red torii gate with its feet in water at high tide.

At Hiroshima, we were briefed about the medical treatment of the atomic bomb casualities. Before going to the memorial exhibits to the bomb victims, I warned Kay-K that the pictures and displays might be gruesome and that she did not have to study them. However, I felt she should go with me. Afterward, we had dinner with the mayor and sat in his box to watch the municipally-owned professional baseball team. Both of us were fascinated as the local baseball boosters ran along the sidelines with brilliantly-colored flags, paper dragons, and fish kites whenever a ball was batted out or a run scored. It was a wonderful Japanese version of the old Brooklyn Dodgers fans and their festivities.

At Kyoto with its ancient palaces and shrines, Kay-K was listed as a "secretary" because youngsters were not permitted to visit the innermost imperial gardens for which special permission had to be obtained to enter. She also could have qualified as "staff photographer" and her pictures proved it.

In the Hakone Lake region, we stayed at a modern hotel with a magnificent view of Mt. Fiji. While resting on a raft after a late afternoon swim, I asked our JNPEA escort what he might have done if he had not been assigned to accompany us for several weeks. He replied that he might have climbed Mt. Fiji, looking up at the peak with what I interpreted as a slightly wistful look. That indication launched a whole expedition. We were going to climb the mountain the next morning. I told Kay-K, who had some doubts, that she was most welcome to go but that if she decided to join us, I didn't want any loud complaining about how tired she was. I added that she might regret it later if she opted out but that the decision had to be hers. We rushed around the village to buy shoes, sturdy pants, and other equipment. We got up around 2 a.m. or slightly later. Kay-K finally decided that she would take pictures of Fiji's summit from the hotel grounds and did not join us. My JNPEA companion and I rode a bus for the first five of the ten stations to summit. After that, it was under each individual's own foot-power. As we were leaving the seventh station, I spotted a building that seemed halfway to the heavens and asked, "What's that?"

My knowledgeable campanion replied, "Station Seven and a Half." I was stunned.

"Damn! How many more half stations are there?"

"None."

After so much puffing that I almost gave up the climb, we reached the summit by early afternoon and branded our walking sticks and the flag that I carried to certify my climb. Coming down was a breeze and I worried that I was making such fast progress with the seven-league boots I seemed to be wearing that I might twist a leg and break a bone. I believe it was less then half an hour from the summit to the bus stop. The way up had been tiring and sweaty, even well above ten thousand feet. Back at the hotel, Kay-K congratulated us and said she had taken some beautiful shots of our climb but unfortunately we would not be able to identify ourselves from the prints when she got them. We would not even show up as dots on the distant mountain side.

When we returned to San Francisco, I was able to fullfill my promise to take Kay-K to a U.S. National Park. We went to Yosemite for an overnight visit. An August dry spell had left no water for the park's precipitous waterfall that looked so beautiful in picture post cards. Did the Japanese manage things better in their national parks? Or what?

Kay-K's arrival at the Northampton School for Girls was Old Home Welcome Week for her grandmother. Not only had the headmistress been her teacher when she had been at a Northhampton school two generations earlier but "Grandma" Lancaster's best friend now headed the business side of the school's administration. Kay-K adjusted rapidly to the new environment, even to learning how to try to get additional money above her allowance. As a single male parent, I had to learn how to counsel our daughter in financial affairs as well as how to behave as a maturing young adult. During a ski weekend in her freshman year, she obtained extra money from me for room, transportation, and board and borrowed second-hand equipment. Like me, she had heard her mother tell of an experience at Smith when a classmate had suggested, "Try tears" to improve a poor grade. I have strong opinions on that score and had explained that I turned extra suspicious when any NYU student tried that approach. However, Kay-K tried tears just once when I declined a phoned request for extra funds. (It was a collect call, naturally.) She began to sob, "Oh, Daddy, please let me have the money." I cut in, "I'm not going to pay my money to listen to you try that treatment on me," and hung up. A couple of minutes later, the phone rang. Kay-K was completely self-possessed. I was so pleased that she had reacted that way that I gave her the extra funds. Maybe she knew me better than I did myself!

One September morning, Kay-K, her grandmother, and I were readying to take her back to Northampton. She was bringing down her clothes and putting them on a rod in the back of our car, while I was reading that morning's copy of the *New York Herald Tribune*. Kay announced that she was ready and I said that we'd take off when I finished reading the newspaper. She exploded, stormed across the room, grabbed the section I was reading, and ripped it in two pieces. I was furious, but kept the emotion buried. Calmly, I said, "All right, here's ten cents; you can go up to the corner store and buy another *Herald Tribune*." She stormed out but came back to report that all the *Tribs* had been sold. We started off but I stopped at neighborhood delicatessen, which, unfortunately for my point-making, also had sold all copies. However, I never again saw such a temper display by my daughter. "Grandma" Lancaster several times recalled the incident and asked how I had controlled my temper. I explained that I had lost it once as a teenager and realized that if two idividuals both got mad at the same time, and if I was one of them, violence just might occur. Kay-K was obviously furious so I had to control myself.

Like her mother, Kay-K liked to cook. One summer, while her grandmother was vacationing with friends in Maine for a couple of weeks, I asked Kay-K if she would help with dinner for a journalism teacher who was preparing to join the NYU faculty. She said, "Sure. You cook the steak over the outside broiler." I was lucky with my broiling and her part of the meal was as professional as a three or four-star restaurant. The new professor was impressed and, later, I heard about the flattering report he gave his own daughters when they arrived in the metropolitan area.

Anxious to involve her grandaughter in cooking, "Grandma" Lancaster offered to wash the dishes "any time" after Kay-K's cooking. My daughter was a real exploiter and I received some complaints from her grandmother in future years, especially after Christmas cooky baking. I had to remind my mother-in-law that she had made an open-ended proposal and would have to renegotiate the deal with Kay-K.

Kay-K was elected to the student council as an upperclassman. She was supportive of a new headmistress whose different ideas upset some of her classmates. She argued that the new faculty member should have a chance to demonstrate what she had in mind and not encounter purely knee-jerk disagreements to any changes.

In her junior year, she won "best student" honors in biology. Her professorial father, who had reported on science and medicine during his newspaper career, was delighted and purchased some science books to add to her personal library.

Despite some early difficulties with her grades, Kay-K was on the scholastic "Honorable Mention" list during her senior year.

During the summer of 1963, Kay-K joined me for a tour of midwestern colleges. I was gathering information for a study of the National Science Foundation's efforts to upgrade secondary school teaching of science and mathematics. While I collected data and interviews, she visited admission offices and picked up application forms. At Northwestern, which she eventually attended, I was surprised that she didn't spend more time sightseeing around the campus. When I questioned her, Kay-K said she had seen enough to know that she liked the school and would apply. (Later, she teased me, saying my graduate degree from Northwestern had helped her get in, which was hardly the case. Her Northampton record, while not spectacular, was not so low that she had to add my degree as part of her credentials.)

Parents' Weekend of her senior year at Northampton ended in a near disaster for the two of us. It had been a pleasant visit until Sunday morning when I had joined Kay-K's roommate's parents and others for brunch at the Lord Jeff hotel in Amherst. We returned to the motel rooms to discover the soon-to-be-graduated students had sampled the liquor supply. Several of the girls were wobbly, and my darling was in the toilet throwing up. To say I was furious is putting it mildly. I really told her how I felt about her performance. I said she had had champagne and wines at birthday parties and why, for heaven's sake, had she tried everthing at once. A queezy voice replied, "Daddy, wouldn't you rather have me get sick now than on a date at Northwestern?" The answer, obviously, was affirmative but it took me a while to calm down. I delivered Kay-K to the school dormitory and saw her safely to her bed so she could "sleep it off." Later, Kay-K herself referred to her actions as a "horror show" in a letter of quasi-apology.

Graduation was suitably ceremonial at the Northampton School, as they almost always are at boarding schools and colleges. Her grandmother and I beamed with proudness. That summer, before she took off for Evanston, Illinois, and the start of her college years, Kay-K enrolled for a world history course at NYU's Washington Square campus and got other credits to go along with her advanced placement biology from prep school.

With all the clothing, record player, stereo speakers, and other necessities for a freshman year, Kay-K and I drove west to Evanston for orientation week and settling her into the dormitory assigned to underclassmen. (In the 1980's, one undoubtedly would say, "underclass persons.") As the University relaxed its *in loco parentis* role, Kay-K moved from the dormitory to a University-managed apartment building to off-campus quarters near the Howard Street boundary with Chicago. When she moved into the campus apartment, she had to obtain my permission. I gave it because apron strings have to be untied. Also, even in the dormitory, if she really wanted to stay out late, she could always arrange to get in with aid from any student who had a key.

During Kay-K's college years, I attended numerous meetings around the country and was fortunate enough to go through Chicago at least several times annually. Thus, I could arrange to visit Evanston or have her come down to Chicago for a chat and a meal.

During one of these visits, we were discussing grades, as parents inevitably do. She explained that she was doing fairly well in all her work except a French course. I asked what was the matter and she replied, "Maybe if I went to class oftener, I'd get better grades."

"What does that mean?" I inquired.

Kay-K responded, "It's an 8 o'clock class and I can't get up that early."

I exploded, "What did you just say?"

We had a lively discussion and it must have had some effect on class attendance because her final French grade was passing.

Because she was born on April 1, Kay-K always could count

on a birthday present at about the same time that Northwestern had its spring "break." And she always asked that her present take the form of cash. Thus, she was able to go on trips with her schoolmates to Nassau, as well as to Aspen and other ski resorts. Despite the size of her birthday gift, I always had to brace myself for a plea for money at the end of each of these trips. One year, she called from Florida and asked me "please" to put money in her bank account to cover checks she already had written in the Bahamas. The request frequently was to take it out of the following month's allowance but that, I found, only delayed the real decision for a month or six weeks.

One financial argument arose when I got a bill from the Northwestern Co-op Bookstore for a few books along with a lot of other, less academic and less necessary, purchases. After a phone discussion with Kay-K and some more specific financial ground rules, I paid the amount and sent a letter to the Co-op, saying that I would no longer be responsible for my daughter's bills. I mailed a carbon copy to her and she never ran up another large bill there.

Kay-K worked summers during the years at Northwestern. She and some of her Mamaroneck friends obtained jobs as waitresses at a resort at Bomoseen Lake, Vermont. While she earned funds for her "pin-money" expenses, she also had the part-time joys of water skiing, tennis, and other sport activities available to the regular guests.

When I went to Vermont one summer to pick up her and her gear, we stopped for food on the way back home. The waitress was incredibly slow, taking one set of orders, placing them, and then delivering them person by person. We were still waiting to have our meals delivered and Kay-K's bitter comments and criticism got so loud that I had to tell her to quiet down. I realized then that she must have been an excellent waitress herself and really deserved the lavish tips that she earned. She said that within a day or two at the resort she knew the favorite foods of all those she served and could have them ready when the guests appeared.

Kay-K left her Bomoseem job early the second year but then wanted to go back to visit some of those who were still on the resort staff. I wanted to see the Montreal Expo so I offered to drive her to Vermont. When I delivered her at the cottage where she was to stay, I found that she was the only girl sharing the place with four young men. I mentally gulped hard, decided I should be a liberated parent, and resolved that my daughter was old enough to manage her own life style. I took off for Montreal. Rethinking the living arrangement as I drove north, I wondered what "Grandma" Lancaster might think of it—if she knew. I decided to return to the cottage. Kay-K greeted me, pixy-smile and all, "I thought you might come back." I told her that I was going to pay for a room at a nearby motel for the period of her visit, ". . . just in case you want to use it."

Having dropped out of her sorority at Northwestern, Kay-K ran as an Independent candidate for Senior Senator on the Student Council. She won. During the fall, she sent me a long clipping relating how several Senators, including my daughter, had gotten into what the student paper described as a "shouting match." In an accompanying letter, she commented that she was sending the clipping so that "at least you'll know that I'm not an obstinate bitch just when you're around."

Before my trip to Chicago for a journalism teachers session in February, 1968, Kay-K wrote, "You are welcome to stay here if you want. If you think you can stand staying with three females, even for so short a time—BUT you *have* to wear pajamas!" I stayed for one night, wearing pajamas, and bought a couple of steaks and, I believe, artichokes, plus a batch of kitchen staples, for the entire group to cook a festive meal. That was their choice instead of having me take them out for an expensive meal.

The year of 1968 was one of the peaks for student demonstrations against the Vietnam war, with the climax coming at the Democratic convention in Chicago. Northwestern students that spring had occupied some administration offices and Kay-K had recorded it on film, including one with students sitting in front of a "Dow Shalt Not Kill" sign. Such an environment was not conducive to good grades. Kay-K invited her grandmother and me to graduation—providing she passed all her courses. The weekend before graduation, I got a telephone call from her, reporting that we could buy our airplane tickets. She had passed everything.

Graduation was the traditional affair with seniors in their black robes and mortarboards and tassels; proud, beaming parents and relatives; faculty and staff with polite smiles that seemed to say, "Yes, we've seen it all before"; marching mobs; "Pomp and Circumstance"—that academic theme song for commencements—and the bestowal of degrees by goups.

Transportation was limited since we had no car of our own there. Walking to a nearby surburban line, Kay-K took off her shoes and went barefoot. "That's much more comfortable," grinned our relaxed recent graduate.

Kay-K chose to stay in the Chicago area for the summer, working part-time as a waitress before she came to New York City for advanced courses at the New York Institute of Photography. That August, I was at a journalism teachers' convention at the University of Kansas and had stayed up most of one night when the anti-war demonstrators clashed with the Chicago police. On the way back East the next day, I called Kay-K from Kansas City to see if she was all right. If she were not, I planned to shift my flight to Chicago instead of New York. All was well. She had photographed the demonstrators early in the week but was busy waitressing when the protests reached the riot stage near the Conrad Hilton Hotel.

Kay-K had arranged to live in New York City while taking her photographic training, but her intended roommate changed plans. As a result, Kay-K decided to live in Mamaroneck and commute to the city. I was both surprised and pleased.

Since both of us were on fixed schedules, we could arrange only infrequently to meet at the University or Grand Central for the train ride home together. When we got to the station platform, however, we would tour the last three or four cars to find each other. One evening, our ride was interrupted when a signal tower collapsed across the tracks and we had to find our way to Mamaroneck by alternate transportation. We called "Grandma" Lancaster to alert her that we would not be on time, found an out-of-the-way restaurant in the Bronx for an excellent dinner, and then took a meandering bus into Westchester County.

We also saw some Broadway shows together. One evening when I had tickets for Marlene Dietrich's revue, Kay-K came to the University office and said she'd like to go, too. At the last minute, I was able to get her a single seat. I was delighted that she was as entranced with Dietrich's performance as I was, although I had many years of nostalgia to my advantage. Another time, I purchased a trio of seats for *George M*, so Kay-K, her date, and I could see that show.

After several months of selling cameras at a Manhattan store, Kay-K argued that she didn't have enough free time to take photographs that she could sell and thus establish herself as a professional photographer. I suggested that she try to find a job with a publication, possibly the Westchester newspapers, but that didn't work out. So she quit her sales job and started taking pictures, both on her own and with another graduate of the Institute. Thus, she was in Ithaca when the black students seized the Cornell student union. Pictures from that demonstration documented the news headline of "Guns on Campus," as *Newsweek* told it. Kay-K called, saying that she was staying on the campus to get more pictures. When she arrived home, I asked what she had done with the prints. "Nothing, yet," she responded. I insisted that news pictures, like ice in the sun, deteriorate rapidly in value and urged her to place them. Black Star agency handled them and, despite the tardy start, was able to sell many of them, especially in European publications. (More than a month after Kay-K's death, *Time* magazine printed one of her Cornell photographs.)

Kay-K joined her Mamaroneck friend, Patti Connor, early in the summer at Lake George. She got a job, again as a waitress, and continued to shoot photographs of that summer resort. She came home to pick up some clothes and other things for the summer and we went into New York to see *Oh Calcutta!* I was intrigued with our reactions to that show which some had criticized for its display of nudity and off-beat sex. Chronologically, I was old enough to be her grandfather but Kay-K and I agreed on most criticisms of the performace. If anything, I think I was, as they say, more "enlightened" than my twenty-three-year-old offspring.

Kay-K left for Lake George, telling me about the wonderful young man she had met there. He certainly must have been important in her life because he got her to give up smoking cigarettes, a goal I had tried to attain for several years.

The end of that month I took off for a trip to the Scandinavian countries. The evening I left I tried for several hours to phone Kay-K to wish her well again and to say goodbye. Later, I found out that the digits in my copy of the phone number had been wrong. I had been calling some empty municipal office. The trip was all booked except for a fjord excursion that was to take place during three of four consecutive days. I loved Copenhagen, with its streets for pedestrians instead of cars and its famous amusement park, and went on to Norway. At a resort hotel at Tyin, an overnight stop, I went for a late afternoon swim in the glacier-fed lake and shivered despite a brisk bath-towel rubdown. After dinner, I watched a group of young tourists cavorting in a bouncy dance and thought of the adage, "Youth is too good to waste on the young." I went to bed and fell to sleep almost immediately. Around 4 a.m., I awoke with a start. What was wrong? Had something happened to my mother-in-law? Or what? I sought to dismiss the feeling and eventually got back to sleep. I rode on to Bergen, where I got up early Sunday morning so that I could tour the Old Town and a mountain amusement park. When I returned to the hotel, I got a telephone message from one of my NYU colleagues.

"Have you heard from anyone yet?" he asked.
"No. What's up?"
"You better call home."
"Don't be cute. What's happened?"

He told me that Kay-K had been killed by a hit-and-run driver at Lake George early Friday morning. Her body had been found after dawn and identified by the young man that she was dating. I immediately dropped all my plans in order to fly home, but airline offices were closed on Sunday night. The first available flight to Copenhagen was late Monday morning. I didn't sleep much that night and I calculated that my sudden awakening the previous night had been an hour or two before Kay-K was hit and killed. Just coincidence or some lurking evil threatening her life? The police never learned who drove the car that hit her.

During the restless dawn hours, I completed the day-by-day diary that I was keeping and ended it with this line from John Adams's despair in the play *1776:*

"Is anybody there? Does anybody care?"

Part Two

KAY KRIEGHBAUM

2. Country Living: Growing-up Years

NEW ENGLAND

Back in the days when the stock market was crashing and the world was trying its best to fall to pieces, I had several good years . . . amusing, rich, soul-satisfying years. Country years are apt to be that, I think, and my years were country ones. My mother and I fled the city for a small New England town, rented ourselves a quite large house with a delightful big barn and grounds for gardens, and let our city-frustrated roots expand deep down in the friendly earth.

Perhaps I am writing this as an effort to keep all the memories that I can intact and fresh; or perhaps it is a wish-fulfillment, since for years after leaving the village I cherished a hope, vain but unadmittedly so, that some day I would go back. I doubt that, now. There is apt to be little going back. Too, perhaps the place where I would return has changed as much as I. Civilization is encroaching on small New England towns, and civilization is something that I prefer at a minimum. A child's dream can shut it out, no matter how close it actually may be, but then the child is child no longer; she cannot go back to the imagined isolation without seeing the asphalt roads and the whizzing motors that profane the countryside and shut out the smell of the fields. She cannot quite rid herself of the horrid knowledge that the casual plowboy in blue denim and old straw hat is of the age to be preoccupied with how many gallons of gas he can afford for the family flivver, the price of cigarettes and beer, a coin for the nickelodeon, and getting done with the chores in time to take his girl to the nearest movie palace where LaVerne L'Amoureuse is to be seen in *Flaming Love* for a quarter on week nights.

I am a sentimentalist about the country, so perhaps I am better trying to see it again from afar as I saw it as a child. If the plowboy spent his evenings lounging on the sidewalk in front of the mill town drug store then, I did not know it. I am glad I didn't. I have no patience with people who urge you to look at reality in the glare of an arc lamp when reality is ugly and there is nothing to be gained by your looking at it. If you can make it less ugly, well and good, look till your eyes hurt. But if there is nothing you can do about it and you only make your own life less lovely by looking, then veil it in the soft light of a candle and let the realists fall where they may.

I have come a long way since first I looked upon the New England countryside and found it beautiful. To date I have never looked and felt the lack of that original charm. When I do, I shall stop going back.

Tonight I am going back only within myself . . . but I find the return pleasant. There is a certain un-copyable glow in returning to years that were full and good. And the years when mother and I lived in the drafty old house and did things with gardens and cats and chickens that reduced the natives to tolerant hilarity, tinged with affection engendered by what they considered our mild insanity, were good years. They were my growing-up years, but I shall hope, now that I am grown, that I can still recapture them in the eyes of the maturing child who lived them.

THE ICE MAN
Summer 1929

Mother and I have made a momentous decision. We are about to buy an electric refrigerator. We have craved one for years, and told ourselves we couldn't afford it. We still can't ... but we are going to get it in sheer self-defense. The ice man has driven us to it.

There are drawbacks to living in the country, and the greatest of these is the ice man. There is but one. He makes three or four trips a week through our village and the surrounding towns and sells good pond ice at a nominal price. We have long regretted that a vague uneasiness as to the probable origin of the ice made it inadvisable to use it in anything. So many people casually swim in their ponds, and let mills use the water, and even drain their plumbing off in that general direction, and then think nothing of selling the ice next summer! But that is not the reason we have decided that the ice man and his product must at all costs be dispensed with. The root of the matter is the ice man's personality.

He is a very friendly soul ... all these people are. But the ice man carries friendliness to rather an excess sometimes. The other day he invaded M's kitchen while she was baking, and took up a good half hour delivering a long monologue on nothing at all. He always acts as though he were a long-lost brother and there are people whom I would prefer as relatives. He goes slowly through the house leaving a trail of wet spots to mark his progress . . . and he has to go all the way through the dining room and kitchen to get to the little back kitchen where the icebox lives. More than ever I wonder at the architect, if any, who achieved this house! I was distinctly peeved at the ice man myself, recently. He came in while I had my typewriter on the dining room table, for purposes of typing a letter and being near the telephone at the same time. And the first thing that heralded the i.m.'s presence was a voice from where he was frankly reading the letter over my shoulder! "Writing to your boyfriend?" inquired the ice man cordially. I cringed . . . more at the term than at the ice man's behavior. If there is one word in the American language that connotes sticky embraces in third-rate movie houses, and similar unpleasantnesses, to me, it is that word "boyfriend." "Girlfriend" is as bad . . . I hope I am not a snob but I do cringe at language that smacks so utterly of the scullery and the slum and the factory.

However, when, my esthetic distaste died down I expressed myself to M. on the subject of the ice man, and she agreed that something would have to be done.

She was a bit lukewarm about it until this afternoon. We had been away for the day, and had left the key to the side door under the corner of the flower box nearest the house, as usual. We always leave it there, so that if Mrs. S should want to get into the house for anything, or if one of us should decide to return before the other, the way will be clear. To the best of our knowledge no one except ourselves and one or two close friends knows the system. We returned, and it was late and hot. M. entered the house bewailing the fact that we had unadvisedly overstayed our time away and so missed the ice man's visit.

With dire predictions of sour milk and melted butter, she went out into the back kitchen to survey the prospect . . . and there, resting peacefully in our ancient icebox, was a large, adequate new iceberg. It most definitely had not been there when we left. The then occupant of the box had been a feeble fragment.

M. blessed our thoughtful neighbor . . . people do such kind things for you in the country. But subsequently, on being thanked, our neighbor disclaimed any part in the matter. More and more mystified, we awaited the ice man's next visit. He brought up the subject himself . . . Yes, he had put the ice there. "But how did you get in?" inquired M. in considerable perplexity. The i. m. responded ingeniously that he had let himself in . . . He knew where the key was! How he knew it we will never know. We eyed each other, speechless. The ice man is doubtless a fine upstanding citizen, endowed with fine upstanding Slavic ancestors, a fat wife, and eleven children . . . but he looks like a broken-down pugilist who goes in for a little light housebreaking on the side. If one did not know his innocuous calling, one would call the police at first sight of him in the kitchen . . . many burglars would no doubt feel more sure of themselves if they were so well equipped by nature to play their nefarious part! The thought of him prowling in solitary state about the place was not reassuring.

We changed the hiding place of the key, after we had weakly thanked the ice man for his thoughtfulness in keeping us supplied with his product! M. is always polite. If ever she had an encounter with a bona fide burglar, I am sure he would tip his hat to her when he finished and she would say, "You are welcome!" Then we looked at each other, cursing that the key was much less convenient in its new abode. Furthermore, how could we ever be sure the ice man would not indulge in some more devining on the side and locate it again? Or perhaps he had some tools for forcing windows . . .

Aware that we were doubtless doing him a grave injustice, we still felt uncomfortable. And then M. settled the matter. We are going to get that electric refrigerator. The young man from the electric shop is even now on the way out here, and in due course (and shortly we hope), we shall dispense with the ice man, his puddles on the floor, his long conversations, and his inconvenient Sherlock Holmes habits forever.

SUMMER 1930

This house is fast assuming all the earmarks of a menagerie. I do not object in the least. I love menageries, so long as they are actual ones populated properly and not, as in city apartments, with assorted specimens of homo sapiens. Naturally, too, I have no objection when the menagerie is largely of my doing. Mother puts up with it like a lamb, but I shudder to think what some of our more proper relatives' reactions would be.

At a tender age I was addicted to the Doctor Doolittle books, and one sentence stays with me. Probably I remember it because at the time a city apartment pretty well frustrated my zoological inclinations and the good Doctor's household filled me with indescribable longings. Anyway, the sentence, as I remember it, catalogued the Doctor's animals, ending up with "white mice in the piano, a squirrel in the linen closet and a hedgehog in the cellar." Well, we may lack a hedgehog, but this morning in similar vein I took a census, with results, *viz:*

A woodchuck in the kitchen, canaries in the living room, a wild mouse on the china cupboard, gold fish in the library, a puppy on the sun porch, and a kitten in the bathroom . . . to say nothing of three big cats at large all over the place, a salamander in a basin in the back kitchen, very young chickens in coops that deface the side lawn, and squirrels in the attic! The latter are quite impromptu . . . we had nothing to do with their coming, and though we have tried to board the place up and have something to do with their going, to date success has not crowned our efforts. They surmount our barriers with absurd ease and quite properly, once their surmounting is done, are more at home than ever, and duly accumulate immense quantities of nuts which they will gaily roll around over our heads on winter evenings. I am convinced that squirrels are addicted to bowling. The reverberations from the attic could arise from nothing else. All winter we live in a state of perpetual quiet-shatterings by athletic squirrels. So the squirrels are a gift of prodigal nature, but apart from them I must plead guilty.

While the locations of the menagerie are all inspired by good sense and purpose of convenience, I have to admit that they are a bit unorthodox. The woodchuck resides in the kitchen because it is an enormous room, and warm . . . the woodchuck needs warmth, being very young. The wild mouse had perforce to be put in the highest available spot. M. drew the line at the book cases in the library, and apart from them only the top of the china cupboard is cat-proof. The puppy's manners are still at that tender stage where it is inconvenient to give her the run of the house unchaperoned, and the sun porch, outdoors but screened, is large, airy, and ideal. Having the puppy on the sun porch means that another habitat had to be found for the kitten, who must be restrained for analogous reasons. The big bathroom boasts both sun and a tile floor . . . the situation speaks for itself. The big cats drift where they may, the fish and birds occupy sunny windows, the chickens had to be installed where there was fresh grass, sunlight, and a convenient view from the house to insure their welfare.

Thus the tale . . . quite out of Doctor Doolittle, and I am still wondering about the effect it will have when visitors from the city descend upon us, impeccable in limousines!

MR. Q

My mother and I decided to move to the country in 1929. For once in our lives, following what seemed to be a general trend at the time, we forthwith rented a house in Connecticut. It was a pleasant house on a hill, at the end of a village street, surrounded by sufficient solitude and ample space for gardens. There was a large barn attached to it, flanked by a delightful orchard stretching down into a little valley that lay between our hill and the next.

On our first tour of inspection we discovered that the near end of the pasture behind the barn held a small, dilapidated shack. A rusty stovepipe protruded crazily above its weathered roof, evidence that the building had once housed heating apparatus of some sort. We contemplated it from the vantagepoint of our new barnyard, congratulating ourselves upon rapid absorption of country lore when we decided, brilliantly, that the pipe must mean an incubator. Chickens—well and good. We were determined to go into this country business thoroughly. Although we had't rented the orchard or the pasture, we decided on the spot to negotiate for the shack and turn it into a proper hen house. But we never acquired that hen house. Instead, we acquired Mr. Q.

That is not his proper initial, but during the early period of our acquaintance with him we thought it was. Local pronunciation led us into the error, and by the time we discovered our mistake it was much too late to change our mode of reference. Always for us he remains Mr. Q.

We had our preliminary glimpse of him on our first night in the village. We were looking out our windows, enchanted by the dusky hills (our neighbors considered this preoccupation with the scenic side of nature one of our chief peculiarities; they never impractically looked at views — they were always rushing out with implements to do something to them) when Mr. Q came shambling around a bend in our driveway.

He was a bent old man, wearing clothes that were intact but obviously in need of soap and water, even to the twilight eye. He had a battered felt hat rammed back on his head, and he was smoking a pipe that we subseqently came to believe was almost as old as he. How often, during the course of seasons when windows stood open to the breeze, we were to curse that malodorous pipe, but of this we were mercifully unaware at its introduction. A battered object, probably a tobacco tin, protruded from Mr. Q's starboard pocket, and he carried a small package which doubtless contained groceries. We watched him until the corner of our fence obscured him, and thought how well he fitted into that rural landscape. Many people would probably have considered him a character. We did not. We flatly refused, when we pulled up our urban roots, to consider anybody a character. Long suffering at the hands (or, rather, the tongues) of acquaintances subject to that affliction had implanted in us an unshakable resolve not to regard anything that had to do with the country, under any circumstances, as quaint.

So we stood at the window, devoid of coyness and adjectives, until Mr. Q. reappeared, carrying a pail and heading, somewhat to our surprise, for our woodshed door. He vanished in the lee of the house. We heard the door bump, then the sound of water splashing from the cellar tap. Curiously we waited as he came back into view with his bucket full, shuffling off around his original corner.

Obviously, he lived very near—not more than five minutes had elapsed between our first sight of him and his reappearance. We wracked our brains to remember the distance of the first house down the side lane. It would have taken him twice five minutes, at least, to go there, deposit his groceries, and return. Besides, that house had a well, eloquent of self-sufficient water supply. The pump might have failed, to be sure—a habit of country pumps, we were to discover—but this performance had borne the unmistakable stamp of custom, not of particular emergency. So matter of fact had been Mr. Q.'s demeanor, such reserved dignity had enveloped him, that we had hesitated to sally forth and accost him. Nevertheless, we had to solve this mystery. Making scathing remarks anent our own curiosity ("So nice to have a party line to listen in on!" we murmured deprecatingly. "And what a pity there's no fence to gossip over with our neighbor beyond the orchard!"), we departed for the latter's house.

Our neighbor greeted us beamingly. She evidenced no suprise when we plied her with questions. "Good gracious!" she ejaculated, agitatedly stroking the cat's fur the wrong way so that it glared at her in disgust and stalked off. How could she have forgotten to tell us about Mr. Q.? So stupid of her! And were we frightened when we saw him go into our cellar? She was so sorry.

No, we weren't frightened, we hastened to reassure her. "After all," remarked mother, "we were two to one, you know, and my daughter used to play with some small boys who had a punching bag in the attic."

Our neighbor greeted this remark stonily. We soon discovered that our private brand of humor had little appeal for these direct, pleasant people. To spare both ourselves and our listeners embarrassment, we learned to deal publicly only in the approach direct, reserving our beloved asides and inverted commas for each other, or a handpicked few.

In our neighbor's immaculate parlor, we steered the conversation hastily back to Mr. Q. himself. We were amply rewarded by the ensuing tale, though it was, as developed during the subsequent months, only a part of the saga of Mr. Q.

He lived in the shack in back of our barn—the "hen house." Our neighbor had eloquent eyebrows as she told us of his domestic habits. Mr. Q.'s ablutions, it appeared, were confined to that part of his laboriously acquired pailfuls that didn't go for culinary purposes. In the winter when the shack was drafty and heating water on the stove required effort, our neighbor doubted that he washed at all. The angle of her nose indicated that Mr. Q.'s pipe was not the only thing about him that profaned atmospheric freshness.

She also expressed the opinion that his clothes were innocent of all water but the rain. That was libelous, we discovered to our considerable amusement the next summer. One afternoon in the social month of August, when pastures turn parched and pink and everyone goes calling in the country, we were escorting a party of city visitors over our domain. We took them into the barn, one part of which then housed a flock of hens doomed to these less personal quarters by Mr. Q.'s occupancy of our "hen house." The city contingent, unimpressed by the barn and unfavorably impressed by the hens, picked their way over the uneven boards a trifle overmeticulously. We wanted them to look out the back barn window at our glorious, hen-inspired blackberry patch, and their fastidiousness annoyed us. Picture our delight, then, when we attained the window, to discover that the gods had prepared for our eyes more than blackberries that afternoon. There, draped on the henyard fence, gray with a grime that no scouring could dislodge, large, intimate, and utterly unembarrassed, were two pieces of underwear—male cotton underwear with dangling long arms and legs. Mr. Q. had been doing his washing! We still remember our visitors' faces with the keenest pleasure. We hastened to refute our neighbor's accusations regarding the state of Mr. Q.'s wardrobe.

Our neighbor, however, held a more serious brief than unfamiliarity with soap against Mr. Q. Solitary though he was, he did not, she informed us that first night, live in the shack without company. Numerous small inhabitants shared his bed and board. It was true, too, deplorably enough. In a later stage of our acquaintance, Mr. Q. several times greeted us in the morning with the information that "the bugs had bit him so bad he didn't get much sleep."

We suggested various sprays and powders at first, but later understood his obliviousness to such suggestions. We saw the interior of his shack, carefully papered with old newspapers, flattened out boxes and similar inspired hiding places, and realized that nothing short of razing the building would do any good.

It was on the occasion of our first Christmas in the country that we were thus enlightened. Mr. Q. had relatives in New York whom he sometimes visited over holidays. When he didn't we always saw to it that a good share of our holiday dinner was deposited in heat-preserving receptacles and rushed down to him. Mr. Q. was touchingly pleased. On that initial Christmas, when we stood in the doorway and things in the dim recesses of the shanty stirred before our horrified eyes—I might be less tactful but more accurate if I said they crawled—I remember that Mr. Q. was moved to give us a present. He had received a box from his relatives. Its contents were spread about, and from somewhere Mr. Q. produced a package of dried figs. Realizing that it was only graceful to accept his gift, we thanked him and retired with the package. It was sweet of him but the figs had been opened! We couldn't even contemplate the idea of eating them after that devastating glimpse of his quarters. We were grateful, but as we conveyed his gift home to its final repository—not our table—we did feel that it should be handled with tongs.

We never shared the general disapproval of Mr. Q., though. We liked him. He upset us far less than he upset anyone else in the village, and his story intrigued us. What, we demanded of our neighbor, did he do for a living? He worked for a farmer in the valley, she told us.

He had had some money once, quite a lot of money by local standards—about two hundred dollars—but his wife had inveigled it away from him. Mr. Q. had married, disastrously, some years before. He had come over from Germany, drifted somehow to our village, and gone to work for a prosperous farmer there. He saved his money, but he married "a no-good, flighty woman," according to our informant. Who she was before the marriage I have forgotten, though I do remember that she wasn't a local product. She bore him two daughters and the family lived in a little house on the valley road. Fire and time have destroyed the house, but Mr. Q. left it before the fire. We used to pass the place frequently on our walks, a pitiful ghost with only a fraction of chimney standing, scattered rocks from the crumbling foundations lying about the dooryard, and wild berry vines fast returning to reclaim the ruins. It was an eloquent reminder of Mr. Q.'s shattered domesticity, for his "no-good" wife, after some years of matrimonial nagging, left him for a performer in a passing carnival. Taking Mr. Q.'s daughters with them, they vanished for over a decade.

Mr. Q. moved away from the little house to his bachelor shack. After a while letters began to come from the woman. Our neighbor knew all about this, because Mr. Q. used to have her answer them for him—he had never bothered to learn to write. The letters expressed dissatisfaction with the carnival performer's manners and mores in general, but particularly with his financial status. Invariably, Mr. Q.'s wife requested money, and since the requests craftily purported to be for the benefit of the children, Mr. Q. never failed to comply, despite our neighbor's protests. Finally, however, he ran out of cash. There was nothing more to send. But he still had his wages, and the town was not greatly surprised when one night there was commotion at Mr. Q.'s shanty. The prodigals had returned—wife and daughters, supplemented by what our neighbor described as "two nasty little circus dogs."

Mr. Q. took them all in, but it wasn't a successful reunion. The shack was small for one inhabitant, let alone four. The woman's disposition had not improved with time, and very likely Mr. Q. had become settled in his solitary existence. At the end of a few weeks punctuated by violent quarrels, the wife again departed, bag, baggage, and dogs. The daughters, now nearly grown, went with her.

The trio went to California from where, our neighbor told us, letters still came demanding money, furnished whenever possible by Mr. Q. in spite of the fact that the daughters have married and the woman has lived with several men who might be expected to effect her support.

At first, we tended to regard Mr. Q. as the faithful victim of a romantic tragedy. I think we exaggerated his emotional capacities. He brought up the subject of his family on occasion, and apparently he regretted them little. It was probably less affection than a stubborn Teutonic sense of duty that prompted his occasional financial contributions to California. As for his never having divorced his erring lady, our neighbor undoubtedly hit upon the proper explanation when she declared that he was simply too lazy. Mr. Q.'s dislike for expending effort upon the various concerns of this world would have elicited approval from an Eastern ascetic.

How he lived was always a miracle to us. Nearly eighty years old when we met him, he still walked the daily two miles and back to the farm where he worked for a gentleman referred to by him as "Wully Charles." (That is by no means the gentleman's name. Mr. Q.'s enunciation was as open to question as that which first led us to misinterpret his own initial.) If the expression "iron constitution" were of recent vintage, I should be inclined to the belief that Mr. Q. must have been the model who inspired it. He is eighty-eight now, and he still works occasionally for Wully Charles, cleaning barns and doing sundry odd jobs about the farm. His recent old-age pension has simplified matters for him a great deal, though. The last time I visited the village he told me that he no longer goes to work on stormy days, or when the roads are deep in snow.

Presumably, however, he still eats the unholy mixtures that used to appall mother and me: no vegetables to speak of, gallons of coffee, and worse—Mr. Q. was addicted to soda pop. Every day during the years we lived next door to him he went to the general store, morning and evening, and each time consumed a bottle of pop. Sometimes in the evening he bought several. Every day, even in the winter when the bottles were kept luke warmly on shelves, innocent of ice!

Another regular purchase of Mr. Q.'s, we discovered to our interest, was snuff. The idea of it fascinated us . . . we felt that with it we stepped backward into the eighteenth century. The proprietor of the store had no such illusions, however. Snuff was a commonplace among the local laboring population, he informed us. They chewed it, a habit he regarded with hygienic distaste. He carried a stock of it in small round tins impressively ornamented with a heraldic design in gilt, and I regret now that I never yielded to the spirit of scientific curiosity that used to make me long to purchase one and sample its contents. Respect for the storekeeper's feelings prevented me, so I left the snuff to Mr. Q., speculating sometimes on its effects as a chaser for soda pop.

The discovery that Mr. Q. had theories about diet startled us, I think justifiably. We had supposed him to be devoid of them, but one day he came to the door and presented us with half-a-dozen oranges. They were large, juicy ones, and oranges were expensive that time of year, so we argued with him: Why didn't he want them? They were lovely—also good for him.

No, Mr. Q. declared, they were not. They upset his stomach. He was going to buy him some bananas.

We used to worry about Mr. Q.'s finances. During the years we lived in the village, we spent considerable time hunting up odd jobs that he could do for us. Jobs there were in plenty, but finding some that were suited to Mr. Q. was no easy matter. His age was part of the problem, but the lion's share of it comprised his mental processes. These can only be described as unique, and the worst of them was that, once Mr. Q. got an idea fixed in his head, nothing could dislodge it. Argue, remonstrate, cajole as we would, Mr. Q., ignoring completely the merits of our case, proceeded exactly as he had thought fit in the first place.

Never shall I forget his conception of kindling for the kitchen stove. We had hired him to split kindling for us because the wood arrived sawed into short lengths and the job of dissecting those seemed better suited to Mr. Q.'s years than the more arduous process of shovelling out our paths. So we shovelled the paths ourselves and turned the matter of kindling over to Mr. Q. We soon discovered that there was little difference entailed in the two decisions. We shovelled paths; we also split kindling. The only distinction lay in the fact that Mr. Q. was unaware of the latter item.

Regularly he arrived and dealt with the wood. Up-ending it firmly on the chopping block he split it, once, down the middle. The resultant halves bore a close resemblance to what a city dealer now supplies in response to orders for "small fireplace logs." Usually Mr. Q. left it at that. Sometimes, if the spirit of enterprise stirred exceptionally within him, he was inspired to divide the halves. Never could we persuade him to do more. We tried our best; we pointed out that even the quarters were about as useful as a telephone pole to start fires with; we took him up to the kitchen and demonstrated. Mr. Q. budged not an inch. So we used to pay him and then sneak down to the cellar after he had gone, to convert his chunks into respectable sticks. We always chopped rather furtively and hoped he wouldn't hear us. As soon as the supply was adequate, we carried it upstairs hurriedly to conceal the evidence. We didn't want to hurt his feelings.

Fortunately, Mr. Q.'s feelings were far from vulnerable, for there were cases where we were forced to be less delicate. The matter of lawn mowing is a case in point. The first fall, we put up with his methods. It was too late in the season for them to do much damage. But in the spring we realized that something had to be done.

Mr. Q.'s lawn mowing was a cumulative process. Even when he tackled the job early on his day off, he never finished it for a week. The various sections grew accordingly in the order of their amputation, and our lawn looked like a relief map of a plateau that rose in several stages. Worse, the plateau had whiskers on it. Mr. Q. was utterly incapable of making the swathes he cut overlap. He invariabley left fringes waving triumphantly between them.

Our lawn was enormous, and when we considered the time Mr. Q. took we made due allowance for his age. Unhappily we were also forced to make allowance for the fact that we paid him by the hour. Finally we had to discontinue his services. We tried doing the job ourselves, but it was a nuisance. Besides, we hated to chop the clover's heads off. We had to risk insulting Mr. Q. by hiring an energetic neighbor boy who enthusiastically polished off the lawn in a single morning, complete even to clipping the edges. (We had never been able to make Mr. Q. see any virtue in that.)

Mr. Q. was unruffled when the boy appeared. He considered it merely one of our eccentricities. However peculiar we may have thought Mr. Q., I am convinced that to him we appeared infinitely more so. He regarded us as a pair of amiable freaks whom Fate had seen fit to deposit practically in his lap, and to whom it was his duty to act as guardian and mentor. We had thought vaguely that we were adopting Mr. Q.; instead, he adopted us. He plied us with advice and admonitions; he chaperoned our every visible act; nothing we did that came to his attention escaped his criticism.

In the winter he supervised the process of banking the house. We thought he actually was going to be useful when he warned us that extra loads of straw would have to be deposited against the north woodshed wall, under the kitchen, where some ill-advised idiot had festooned our water pipes. Mr. Q. and the lawn-mowing boy built a sort of manger a foot deep along that wall and packed it with leaves and straw. (I should say, the boy built it. Mr. Q. was usually to be seen during the process, squinting busily along the top of a board to discover its exact line—which didn't matter a particle—or picking up tools, holding them fondly for a while, and then handing them to the boy with accompanying directions.)

The structure upset our architectural sensibilities, but it

looked disarmingly frost-proof. Nevertheless, every night all winter that we forgot to preface our going to bed by an arctic trip down cellar to drain those pipes and shut off the downstairs water supply, the pipes froze. Frequently they burst. Then, as in all domestic crises, Mr. Q. appeared to supervise. While plumber wrestled with the tools of his trade or a man with a blow torch thawed out pipes that were so solid we couldn't melt them, Mr. Q. stood helpfully by, making suggestions which we prized highly because they were so consistently unproductive.

In the summer he concentrated on our gardens. Those we thought we knew something about, and we usually ignored his comments stonily (though mother did form a habit of rising at six to hoe her vegetables without benefit of his judicial gaze).

One particular horticultural episode stands out in my memory. I had rashly converted a large half-moon shaped patch between the curve of the driveway and the terrace into a flower bed. The driveway ran downhill there, and every rain washed its packed pebbles and ashes over into the lower corner of my garden. I tried various kinds of flowers, always without success. I might go out as soon as the rain stopped and rake off the debris, still there was something about the stuff that killed the plants. Finally I hit upon a solution.

Our predecessors on the place had been prone to horrible combinations of golden glows and magenta phlox. The latter we slew unmercifully, but the golden glows were so bushy and enthusiastic that we hesitated to yank them up, despite an intense dislike of their kind. Since they are so tough that they thrive almost anywhere, I decided to try them in the fatal end of my garden. If they didn't grow, nothing would; if they died, we wouldn't mourn them.

It was late September when I moved them. Mr. Q. was absent for the day at Wully Charles', but when he came home that night he duly noted the new arrangement. He sought me out and predicted dire consequences.

"Them flowers," prophesied Mr. Q. " can't live out the winter. It's too late to move'em. They won't be set by frost, and they'll die."

I said heartlessly that I didn't care. I also defended my gardener's pride by proclaiming that I was sure he was wrong. They wouldn't die at all. Unmoved, Mr. Q. repeated his forebodings.

The next spring (and, indeed, every spring thereafter) the allegedly doomed golden glows appeared in the lower end of my garden. They flourished madly. I had to keep pruning them and weeding them back to their original boundary or they would have choked out everything else. We remarked their presence with amusement, hoping for comments from Mr. Q., but for weeks he ignored them as though they had come wearing helmets of invisibility. Then one morning I was on my knees in the border, busily slaughtering their too numerous young, when a shadow fell across the garden. Mr. Q. stood behind me, registering a dispassionate curiosity. Firmly I sat back on my heels to confront him. Tactless or not, I had things to point out to Mr. Q. regarding my judgment of the preceeding autumn.

"They seem to be doing all right, don't you think?" I interrogated.

Mr. Q. said nothing. His expressions were always hard to read, but I fancied he looked puzzled. I indicated the pile of uprooted young plants beside me.

"They spread so—have to keep pulling'em up."

Mr. Q. looked straight through me. "They was transplanted too late!" he said.

"But look at them!" I objected. Mr. Q. looked. He shook his head. Me he disregarded; he looked at the stocky plants with something like awe. He removed his hat, turned it around in his hands three times and replaced it—always a sign of deep cogitation. Obviously he considered the responsibility for the exhibits before him far outside the scope of my powers. Mr. Q. was contemplating the ways of a miraculous Providence.

"They was transplanted in September!" said Mr. Q. in reverent tones. "Ain't never seen nawthin' like it!" And he departed.

Silently I watched him go. There are times when argument is especially futile.

I thought he might interpret the incident to indicate that the powers that be were on my side, and so discontinue his tutorial role, but such far pursuit of logic was beyond Mr. Q. He continued to supervise our gardening, and above all he gave us a course on how to treat our hens. We had to admit that we were rank amateurs where that flock of experimental hens was concerned, and Mr. Q., aware of this, pounced gleefully upon his opportunity.

Every detail of the preparation of their quarters exacted comment from Mr. Q. Once they were installed, he gave us lectures on their diet. Regularly, he noted the size and quantity of the eggs they eventually produced. He discoursed at length upon methods of dealing with Em'ly, a pathetic fowl whose thwarted passion for maternity led her to brood bad-temperedly for weeks in a nest box containing a china egg and a small pyrex custard-cup, put there as a drinking dish for a previous occupant whose efforts to raise a family from more conventional embryo we had seen fit to encourage. No one familiar with *The Virginian* will wonder about the derivation of Em'ly's name.

Mr. Q. advocated direct action in Em'ly's case. We refused to let him immerse her for hours up to her stomach in water (the way, he said, to prevent the desire to "set"), but we finally acted on his compromise suggestion of a very small pen outdoors. Em'ly duly became discouraged, and Mr. Q. directed us more than ever.

He was particularly inspired the sad summer that our hens fell prey to some strange disease. We never knew what it was, for local diagnoses varied. All we knew was that the hens' legs buckled under them; they were unable to stand or to stay on roosts, and their dying was a slow process filled with agony. We tried everything. Only one hen that was stricken ever recovered. Following the suggestion of a neighboring farmer, we had plied her with what our grocer called "red hen-pills." They were murderous looking things, shaped like miniature sausages, dark red, over an inch long, thick as my little finger. To administer them, you clutched the hen under your left arm, pried her beak open and held it that way with your left hand; then with your free right hand you poked the pill as far as possible down her throat and poured water from a pitcher in after it to wash it down, hoping prayerfully all the while that she wouldn't choke.

We were sure the pills would prove more fatal than the disease, but for our test case, whom we dubbed "Susie," they worked. Susie returned to health; but she was a changed creature. Our grocer, when we indelicately put the matter up to him, swore the pills could have no glandular effect. Nevertheless, something happened to Susie's sex. She didn't actually become a rooster; she stood oddly at the crossroads. Her comb remained the same, but her wattles grew amazingly; her voice wasn't a crow, but it was hoarse and too sustained for a cluck; her walk wavered between a scuttle and a stride; she grew long, luxuriant pantalettes as a concession to femininity, but she never laid another egg in her life. Altogether she was an odd creature, and very tame, so that we were deeply attached to her. Susie's tragic demise was our most serious grievance against Mr. Q.

When the epidemic spread and we couldn't cure the sufferers, we arranged to have Mr. Q. dispose of them for us. There seemed no point in letting them undergo agonies when we were unable to help. Mr. Q. accordingly became our Lord High Executioner, and so long as we delivered up the victims personally all was well. Then one day we found a hen in the last stages, just as Mr. Q. was leaving for work in the morning. He hadn't time to attend to her. He promised to do so at the end of the day, so since both mother and I were to be out that afternoon, we explained in great detail what we wanted him to do.

The hens' side of the barn was divided into two rooms, the

big one where they lived and a small vestibule where grain chests were stored.

"If this creature is still suffering when I go out," mother told Mr. Q., "I'll put her in the vestibule—here," she showed him, "and leave the outer door open. I'll shut the door between the rooms so you won't need to go into the main room at all. Just take the hen away, and please shut the outside door after you." (We had had melodrama with skunks when that door was forgotten.)

In the afternoon mother made the scheduled arrangements and departed for her tea, elegant in georgette and floppy hat. Returning, she met Mr. Q. in the drive. He'd put the hen away, he told her. Watching him go off, mother decided that he had also undoubtedly forgotten to shut that vital door. She went out to investigate. The door stood open—and inside on the floor was the sick hen, exactly as she had left it, its breath rattling with effort, its eyes bulging. Mother stared. Mr. Q. had definitely killed something—but what? And how had even Mr. Q. been so stupid as to ignore directions and overlook this invalid?

Misgivings seized her. The door into the main room was ajar. Susie, the pet hen, unable or disinclined since her illness to spend the night on roosts, always slept on the floor by the nearest wall. She was not there. Mother searched the room. Susie had vanished. Mr. Q. had walked straight past the designated bird into the room where he had been told not to go, had found a hen on the floor, and duly annihilated her. Regret for Susie and rage at Mr. Q.'s stupidity overwhelmed mother. She stalked out, slamming the door. The sick hen lay before her, agonized. Something had to be done about it. Mother couldn't bring herself to fetch Mr. Q.—she was too annoyed with him. Firmly, my small mother who dislikes all forms of slaying, who averts her eyes from mousetraps, picked up that hen. Straight to the chopping block she marched, georgette, floppy hat, and all. Ordinarily, she couldn't even have contemplated the deed, but sheer fury accomplishes remarkable things. With one swing of the axe she banished the hen from an unkind world. Still attired for tea, she got a shovel and a basket and buried the corpse out in Mr. Q.'s pasture.

That I missed that scene will remain one of the major regrets of my life. I could hardly believe it—but mother is a truthful woman. She was hurt when I howled with laughter. "It was the only humane thing to do with that hen!" she explained.

When I got my breath, I demanded to know what she had said to Mr. Q. Mother went up like a rocket.

"Mr. Q! That old imbecile!" she exploded. "I didn't say anything to him! I didn't dare go near him—I was so mad I'd have had him on the chopping block next! And I'm not going to say anything to him, either," she finished more mildly. "I really couldn't trust myself to be polite!"

True to her statement, she never did, but on a later occasion when Mr. Q. demonstrated a comparable brand of mental prowess she did attempt to say something to him. I woke one morning to see clouds of smoke pouring out beside the barn. Rushing downstairs, I confronted an alarming spectacle. We had left a pile of leaves and brush in a corner of the barnyard. Damp on the outside from recent rains, it had begun to smoulder inside. Now it was burning hard, with suffocating waves of smoke pouring up from it and little points of flame beginning to poke out of its interior. Mother phoned our neighbors while I collected a hose and a pitchfork. We pulled the mess apart, shooting water into it to keep it from spreading until the men arrived. They were the better part of an hour getting it out.

When the smoke lifted, we saw how great our danger had been. The brushpile had stood beside the barn; two of the big barn posts were badly scorched, while a projecting timber showed a charred end that would have ignited the entire barn if we had been twenty minutes later in discovering the fire.

As the men dispersed, a thought struck us. Mr. Q. must have gone to work as usual just before 8 o'clock. He would have passed the brush pile, not more than fifteen feet from it, only a few minutes before I looked out and saw those waves of smoke. Why on earth hadn't he given the alarm?

Mother went out to meet him when he came ambling down the drive that night. She decided to give him the benefit of the doubt and phrase the question cautiously.

"Did you know we had a fire this morning?"

Mr. Q. looked interestedly at the barn. "Yass," he said, "I saw the smoke. If there'd been anybody around I'd of told ya."

As usual, Mr. Q. had the last word. Speechless, we let him go. Not for us to interfere with the workings of that astounding brain!

Our years in the country ended on a note of tragedy that left us poorer in a great many things, but richer by a climactic, unforgettable episode in the saga of Mr. Q. We had a second fire, when our house burned down in mid-January, at 2 o'clock in the morning. How the fire started we never found out. The subsequently investigating insurance company, unwilling to admit defeat, entered "defective wiring" firmly in its little black book. It may well have been that—the wiring, largely owing its existence to the efforts of a series of local semi-amateurs, was defective enough. We had cursed its machinations for years, recognized it as a grave danger, and talked of having it overhauled by an imported expert whenever finances allowed—which they never did. Remembering the formidable lengths and loops of wire which had festooned our cellar, mother and I inclined to support the insurance company's thesis.

A second school of thought held unshakeably to the more romantic belief that the blame should be attached to a tramp in the woodshed. The woodshed played cellar to our kitchen, and no lock had ever defaced its doors. Hence, argued the dramatic contingent, the conflagration was obviously the work of a tramp and a cigarette butt tossed carelessly among shavings and sawdust.

Aware that the lockless door had also boasted complete absence of glass in its diamond shaped window, mother and I tended to scout this theory. The hypothetical tramp and his cigarette were all very well for the newspapers, but we were sure no tramp, however hypothetical, would deliberately choose to spend the night in a place whose temperature matched the zero air outside while most of our neighbors could have furnished him with warm, beast-filled barns, equally unguarded.

The controversy over the fire's origin has gradually settled into part of our local legend. One thing I do know: The three coal fires, two furnances, and the kitchen stove, were entirely blameless. When, with everyone safely roused, I burst out of the scorching smoke to run down the snowy path to our neighbor's telephone (ours was ten feet from a flaming wall and too hot to touch), I looked back, like Lot's wife, and saw the kitchen windows, glaring red and the ell roof falling in, clouds of smoke pouring from the gaping hole, but only a thin, conservative thread issuing from each of the chimneys, all of which stood forward where the fire had not yet reached.

Our neighbor set to work at the telephone, rousing all the village's available men. (We had no fire department, and the nearest one, five miles away, refused to leave its town limits.) Hurrying cars began to arrive, disgorging hastily-dressed volunteers. There was nothing to be done for our house. Its wooden frame, with a stiff northerly gale fanning the fire, went up like a torch. Ten minutes after we woke, walls and roof were gone; even the chimneys were crumbling.

But a big barn, filled with hay, which stood across the road, demanded attention and a crew of men stayed on its roof all night to put out the flaming brands the wind carried there when our barn caught fire. Later, they told us that blazing bits of wood were blown over the Academy steeple—a distance of three city blocks!

The heat was unbelievable. Our neighbor's house, where we went to borrow something to supplement our night clothes, was a hundred yards away and the wind blew from it to the fire—but the window panes on the nearest side of that house were hot to touch.

Gradually the nightmare wore itself out. The blaze, with everything consumed, settled back to satiate coals; reporters and news photographers had come and gone; the curious went home to bed. At 5 o'clock in the morning, the last cup of coffee had been dispensed in our neighbor's kitchen to the last exhausted volunteer fireman. Mother, our neighbor, and I went out to view the ruins.

A small knot of men still stood on the scene contemplating the smouldering cellar hole. A heavy pall of smoke drifted above them, and a cloud of steam, escaping from a melted and twisted radiator pipe to give evidence that our biggest furnace, ironically enough, was still doing its job, mingled with the smoke. The remants of our winter's coal pile glowed red in the gray half-light like some huge, diabolical eye. The wind had died down ("Nothing more for it to play with," we muttered bitterly) and the thick air was painful to breathe.

The men were fairly visible now; it was nearly dawn. Halfway up the snowy path we stopped dead, all struck at once by a horrible thought. Desperately we peered at the hazy figures; wildly we stared at each other. "Mr. Q!" we gasped, and made for those men at a dead run.

He wasn't there. Nobody had seen him. The men, our consternation spreading across their faces, all declared that he hadn't been around all night. Nobody had seen him since the evening before—nobody had thought of him since we discovered the fire. His shack was a bare fifty feet behind the wreck of our barn—the wind would not have been directly toward it, but it wouldn't have been away from it, either. Barn and shack had stood in direct line in the face of that wind—and the hay-crammed barn had been the most blazing inferno of all. Remembering our neighbor's windowpanes, we stared frantically through the dim light. His shack was right behind the barn—was? Or had been?

It was! Miraculously, unbelievably, that disreputable little structure was still standing. Its angular stove-pipe stood jauntily out against the snow-covered hills, visible across the smouldering ruins like a child's forgotten hobby-horse in a dooryard torn by bombs.

We breathed again. And then a new fear struck us—the heat! The temperature was sub-zero, but in this air, sultry with steam and smoke, we were uncomfortably warm in our heavy coats. Mr. Q. must sleep like the dead. How, otherwise, could the roaring flames, the rending timbers, the motors and horns and shouting men, have failed to rouse him? Someone had even rung the Academy bell, madly, forcing its venerable mellowness into clanging frenzy to tell the surrounding countryside that here on the hill was chaos. Could he have slept through that? Or had he slept like the dead, indeed?

"He must have roasted alive!" mother gasped.

"Or smothered," whispered our neighbor tonelessly.

Mr. Q. always nailed the shack's single window tight at the first frost. If any of that sickening smoke had managed to seep in, how could fresh air have come to counteract it? Had he been stifled as he slept?

Frantically we forced ourselves to action, rushing down the path to the pasture gate. From there, he hadn't bothered to shovel himself a route. Eloquent foot-holes in the snow marked his comings and goings since the last storm. Two of the men plunged across the drifts to his door. The rest of us stood there at the path's end, frozen with a cold more fearful than the January dawn. We didn't want to daunt those drifts—we didn't want to see what those men were going to discover behind that rickety door.

"Perhaps—perhaps he isn't there at all! Maybe he went away for the night, somewhere!" Mother's statement was like a plea. Nobody bothered to answer it . . . nobody believed it. She didn't, either.

We stood there, hypnotized, watching the two men. They had reached the door. They knocked louder . . . taut nerves beginning to fray, they banged on Mr. Q.'s door till the whole shack quivered. They shouted his name, stepped back, shoulders braced for the rush that should smash the door in. And then—it opened—hospitably, from inside. Fumblingly, Mr. Q. pulled his door open. Perplexedly, he peered at us all. There he stood, completely unresentful of this daybreak intrusion, mildly surprised, much too sleepy to assimilate such an unprecedented visitation. Relief flowed over us. We simply stared. Possibly, if he were awake enough to function mentally, he thought us rude. Mother and I clutched each other, unbelieving. He was there—he was alive—he was completely unharmed. And incidentally he was confirming to the letter our longtime suspicion that he slept in his underwear. Grimy and disreputable in his absurd garment, he eyed us amiably.

"My God!" whispered one of the men before him. However often in his life that man had misused the expression, this time it cannot have offended the ear of the addressee. It had reverence. The man was proclaiming a miracle.

His fellow recovered faster. He looked from Mr. Q. to the scene of the fire, and back again to Mr. Q. He couldn't stand it.

"Christ, man!" he burst out. "Have you been sleeping here all night? Don't you know there's been a fire? Look at that!" He pointed sweepingly. Mr. Q.'s sleep-befuddled eyes followed the indicatory finger. He blinked. He took a step forward and scratched his head. Somehow he found his tongue.

"Waal!" said Mr. Q. "I ain't never seen nawthin' like that! Never!"

Admiration and respect vied with amazement in his tones. Then as the full import of it sank in he glanced hastily at the group on the path. Searchingly, he studied it till he found mother and me.

"Waal!" said Mr. Q. again. "Are ye all right?"

We were all right, we told him—and we were so glad he was. At that, Mr. Q. looked mildly startled. He didn't understand it. His house hadn't been afire. He was baffled. Mother and I were quite unable to go into the matter with him. Weak with relief, we simply leaned against a supporting snowdrift and looked at him. But the men who had unearthed him were still unsatisfied. The air of the shack, they told us later, was thick with smoke and heat. It had hung sickeningly behind Mr. Q. when he opened the door. The barnward side of the little building was scorched, and the door, after winter hours, was still tepid to the touch.

"Didn't the smoke bother you?" the men demanded. "What about the heat? Didn't you even notice it?"

A slow pleasure tempered Mr. Q.'s owlish gaze. He nodded thoughtfully. "Yaas . . . it was comfortable," said Mr. Q.

The men by the door goggled at him. The men on the path followed suit. Our neighbor said, "Well! I never!"—in the voice of one who has gazed on wonders and found them, not only wonderful, but also not wholly to be approved. But mother and I looked at each other and then from our hearts we smiled at that ridiculous underwear-clad figure. The nightmare of the past few hours evaporated. We loved Mr. Q.—it was so nice of him to give us something to smile about. And our smiles held, besides thanks, complete comprehension. We understood perfectly. The rest might be astounded—they might repeat the tale for months to come and never find a satisfactory explanation, but in the light of our years with Mr. Q. we were wiser than they. Comfortable? Certainly. Mr. Q's remark was quite natural; in fact, anything else would have been out of keeping. It was perfectly clear. Mr. Q. had thought it was a nice, warm night.

3. City and Suburban Years

SOME FELLOW WASHINGTONIANS

[1957?]

Senator Richard Neuberger's remarks about the removal of White House squirrels distressed me. Hoping that he has been misinformed, but fearing that he hasn't, I should like to enter a plea for the small creatures. I was a fairly close neighbor of theirs for ten years. I enjoyed them, and it's too soon for them to have to leave home again. I'd hate to see them go.

It is less than fifteen years since they (or, rather, their forebears) had their lives disrupted. There was a movement of White House squirrel population then, voluntary, to be sure, but necessitated by circumstances that squirrels could neither control nor understand. I'd like to see the descendents of those displaced squirrels permitted to live peacefully in their ancestral place.

I've never seen it mentioned in print, that squirrel exodus. Senator Neuberger probably does not know about it. He was not in Washington at the time—like many men of his generation, he had urgent business elsewhere for several years. (So did President Eisenhower.) I remember the migration of the squirrels because I had long been fond of them, and I spent those years in Washington.

It happened in the bleak, gray initial weeks of 1942. Like the rest of us, White House squirrels found their lives sharply changed. For years—probably for as long as there has been a White House—their tribe had flourished on its grounds. In my early Washington days they waxed fat on tribute proffered by passersby—sightseers, Sunday strollers, and people going to and from their jobs. Customarily, many of these transients bought bags of peanuts from Steve, the peanut man, for distribution to the little gray rodents who poked anticipatory faces through the iron fence that runs behind 1600 Pennsylvania Avenue.

In the space of one December Sunday, all that was changed. The sidewalk was closed to everyone except armed guards and specially authorized White House callers. Usually it was unoccupied save for a progression of sentries equipped with rifles. And sentries walking post do not carry supplies of squirrel fodder; they couldn't unbend to distribute it if they did.

I lived then just off lower Connecticut Avenue, near enough to my office to walk to it often, cutting down through Lafayette Park opposite the White House grounds. For a while after December 7, 1941, I saw squirrels across Pennsylvania Avenue peering distressfully at a changed world. Curiously they contemplated heavy-booted sentries; obviously they wondered why nobody came to see them any more; hopefully they waited for life to return to normal.

When it didn't, they moved. It seemed as though they must have done it over a single weekend. One Saturday, Lafayette Park held its usual small complement of squirrels; on Monday, it was alive with them. People were hurriedly busy but the park squirrels, occasionally at least, still got fed. The White House squirrels accordingly took up temporary war housing there. A few die-hards remained visible in their old haunts, but the majority moved across the street for the duration. They must have found life crowded—but didn't we all?

In the fall of '45, they went back home. I don't know whether that was a mass movement or a slow trickle back. I was living nearer the city's outskirts then. I remember, though, walking along the newly re-opened sidewalk in back of the Executive mansion. (That it is the back has always seemed paradoxical to me. It feels as if it ought to be the front.)

Squirrels in force crowded inside the fence, anticipating handouts. The park contingent was depleted, reduced to normal peacetime strength.

Shortly thereafter my husband, my Washington-born daughter, and I left our adopted city. I assume that the squirrels stayed. I've thought of them from time to time, wishing them well. My daughter has heard about them and about their wartime exile across an avenue. She is old enough now so that we have been contemplating a trip to reintroduce her to her natal city. I'd hoped that then she, too, could feed squirrels on an Executive sidewalk. Steve, the peanut man, is gone, but probably he has a successor. I'd hoped to take Muffy [family nickname for our daughter] down through Lafayette Park to see a historic house and find it more friendly by feeding small, familiar creatures who live in its grounds. It never occurred to me that they wouldn't be there, poking furry faces through gaps in an iron fence.

There are too many iron fences or their equivalents in this world nowadays. Far more than we anticipated in those hopeful months when three dictatorships surrendered and men—and White House squirrels—began to come home. It has been good to think, in the years while those mid-'40 hopes have proven too high, that passersby—sightseers, Sunday strollers and people going to and from their jobs in one of the world's capitals—could push peanuts through an important iron fence to friendly small creatures who expected only kindness from them. It is good to think that an iron fence anywhere can still be used that way.

So I should like to add my plea to that of the junior Senator from Oregon. I hope that the present highly esteemed but temporary tenant of 1600 Pennsylvania Avenue can see his way to live harmoniously with what I have believed to be his more permanent small fellow dwellers there.

THE LADY GHOST

For almost two years during World War II, I shared an apartment on lower Connecticut Avenue in Washington with a ghost. I also shared it with my friend Toni, whose tenancy preceded mine, and with two temporary roommates. For the better part of a year, while Toni was away in the South, the ghost and I lived there alone together. At least, I suppose we did. It didn't manifest itself until several months had gone by, but it is reasonable to assume that it was there all the time. Its tenure antedated ours. In fact, it was indirectly the reason for Toni's taking the apartment in the first place.

Coming to Washington late in the '30s, Toni set out to find a good apartment, near downtown, with rent suited to a limited budget. Such treasures were not then as rare as they have since become but they were not precisely plentiful.

After considerable discouragement, Toni heard from a chance acquaintance somewhere in the neighborhood of Dupont Circle that there was a whole building vacant a couple of blocks up the street. Rent would be cheap enough, at least for the first hardy soul who dared to move in. The place had recently been the scene of a particularly messy murder: A man who believed, rightly or wrongly we never knew, that his resident mistress had beeen unfaithful, barged into the hall of her apartment one night and shot her. The other tenants, dodging notoriety and scandal, moved out. Ownership of the building changed hands, but the new owners (one of Washington's largest real estate firms) had, so far, a semi-white elephant on their hands. There was a little dry cleaning shop on the first floor, and an office supplies firm with headquarters on the second, but the apartments on the third, fourth, and fifth stood empty.

Toni went to look immediately. The third floor front, enormously high-ceilinged and inconveniently arranged, didn't suit her. The third and fourth floor backs were too small as were the rooms on the fifth. But the fourth floor front was exactly what she was looking for. Murder or no murder, she took it on the spot.

It was a pleasant apartment. The entrance hall compared in size to many living rooms, the living room was large and airy, with long French windows opening on a tiny ornamental wrought iron balcony, the bedroom was equally big, closets and bath were adequate, and best of all from her point of view—and, later, mine—the kitchen was almost as big as the living room.

The fact that this paragon of a dwelling was also the "murder apartment" didn't throw Toni. Two deep bullet gouges that no one had ever bothered to repair, one in the hall floor and one in an inner hall door, merely made good conversation pieces. After I moved in, we added a dart board on the door at the far end of the hall and provided, I'm afraid, a fine collection of small supplementary gouges of our own.

Toni went South in the fall of '43. For a time, I had a temporary roommate. It was shortly after she left, early in 1944, that my non-corporeal roommate's presence dawned on me. This wasn't because I was alone in the apartment; it continued very much with us after Toni's return. It was simply because I like hard beds.

I am one of those quiet sleepers who gets comfortably settled in place and then stays there all night. (Our cat currently provides testimony to this. Despite my daughter's best efforts to adopt him as bedfellow, and regardless of the fact that my husband's bed is in a less drafty spot, our cat glues himself nightly to half my feet. Obvious reason: The rest of the family wiggle and kick. I don't.)

This has its drawbacks. If the mattress is the kind that lets me sink into it, I wake up regularly with an assortment of aches and cramps. Toni's bedroom mattresses were the sink-in kind. There was no way to avoid them with more than one person in residence; nobody wants to bring a late date in for a nightcap and find somebody sleeping on the living room couch! But as soon as I was alone, I adopted the couch. It was wonderfully comfortable, quite unlike the usual instruments of torture. I continued to use it even after I discovered that the living room was the ghost's stamping ground, though at first that took some doing.

I wasn't home much in those days. My job at the War Shipping Administration, to which I had brought scant qualifications or experience, took twelve hours or more a day: eight hours to do what I was hired for, the rest for research in the office library and files to find out what it was all about! Then, I was in love with an Anglo-Irish colonel on the British Army staff whose hours were as long as mine, or even longer, so that our dinners took place at 9 or 10 o'clock, and if we went dancing, as we usually did, the "evening" lasted until around 2 a.m. By the time I hit the studio couch, I needed my sleep. But I found that I wasn't going to get it.

Noises were no novelty in that apartment. Streetcars changing gear to go up the hill above Florida Avenue whacked and groaned; streetcars going the other way clanged hysterically down to Dupont Circle. Numerous late restaurants and bars on the Avenue disgorged noisy patrons at all hours. Taxis took the hill more and more noisily as the war went on and they grew older.

Our aging building vibrated particularly to the street cars. I think I must have mistaken the ghost's operations for streetcar-induced noises for some time. But one night—or rather, one early morning—I was waked by a series of creaks that couldn't be accounted for in any customary way. A wicker rocking chair about ten feet from my bed was going merrily, and there wasn't a breath of wind stirring nor a vehicle audible in the street!

We had two of those wicker chairs, inherited from Toni's mother's sun porch. One straight, one rocker, they were the bulgy, cushioned sort everybody had in the early '20s: really quite comfortable, but awfully noisy to sit in.

I remember rolling over and trying to get to sleep again (usually no chore in those days) without success. The chair was making a fearful row. Finally I got up and closed the windows, even though I couldn't feel any breeze. The chair kept on going. There hadn't been a street car for fifteen minutes. Heat, at that hour, was definitely off so I couldn't attribute this voluble activity to vibrations in the steam pipes. Besides, our janitor, who lived in another building around the corner, had never been known to make 3 a.m. visits. He was an agreeable man who did his job adequately, but "adequately" was the most you could say for him. (In the matter of hot water, you couldn't often say that.) Aging, perennially weary, father of many children, he was unimaginable as a source of activity at such an hour.

Nobody in the building seemed to be moving, either. In fact, nothing was moving but that possessed chair. The reason why we had the apartment, of course, suddenly occurred to me like a blow. I suppressed a strong desire to dive for the bedroom and pull covers over my head.

Eventually, it stopped rocking. Being young, healthy, and thoroughly tired, I went to sleep. But I found the episode very much with me in the morning.

I am not, I hope, unduly superstitious. But there are things I don't understand and don't expect to, and I give them the benefit of the doubt. I have had a feeling of unexplained presences, sad or happy, in too many old houses to be blithely materialist on the subject of the supernatural. I have waked in a strange bed, with my back hair quivering like a dog's or cat's, half-smothered by a sensation of sheer malice nearby, and discovered the following morning that the guiding spirit of that house once was a venomous old woman whose history made Lady Macbeth look like Pollyanna. I don't know why some old places make me feel so happy, so good all over, while I can't wait to get out of others. I never bothered to try to figure out—I know I couldn't—why I once went into the cellar of an old house where I had never been before in my life and told my hostess, till that evening a stranger to me, "The secret subcellar you've wondered about is just behind that wall." They dug, and it was. Spiritualists and mediums annoy me, and I have a vague idea that things like extrasensory perception are better simply accepted than analysed and card-catalogued, so I have never pursued the subject. But that chair scared me half out of my wits.

TROPICAL FISH AS A HOBBY
or,
TAKE AWAY THAT GUPPY!

Tropical fish, says the author of a book we own which is devoted to their care, are ideal pets. They are clean, quiet, non-demanding; no special knowledge is necessary to maintain them at a high standard of health and, presumably, happiness; their culture is a pleasant pastime requiring little time and effort; an elevating, therapeutic hobby, especially suitable for children and invalids.

I should like to meet that man. I'll bet I could make him eat his words. I should be tempted further to suggest that he eat eleven small tropical fish in varying stages of disrepair, a dozen or so assorted snails, one lethargic freshwater mussel, numerous algae-ridden plants with impressive Latin names, a half-bushel of disinfected sand, and one ten-gallon tank complete with steel stand, reflector, filter, and pump. He could wash it all down with beakers of aquarium water which may have acquired therapeutic value from the doses of fish remedies and tonics it has absorbed. (The more expensive were said to contain Aureomycin.) I can think of things he could do with his book, other than consuming it.

The most restrained comment I am capable of making upon all this, is that its author is either a demon for research with no more than a nodding acquaintance with his subject —occasional glimpses, say, in a dealer's window—or else he is a liar of a caliber which should make Ananias immediately relinquish his laurels.

I should very much like to know if this aquarist considers cleanliness an accurate description of conditions which require daily clean-up operations (with a small suction affair known as a dip tube, and weekly struggles with a siphon that removes from the tank bottom both odoriferous dark debris and masses of sand, the latter of which has to be washed and replaced). I wonder if he has ever had the quiet of his home shattered for twelve hours daily by the muted roar of the electric motor which powers the filter necessary to aerate the tank. I question the amount of pleasure to be derived from cleaning the apurtenances of this filter—the glass wool that occupies the top portion of this filter, or the activated charcoal that fills its bottom. If he has discovered any simple method of scouring accumulated slime out of the minute plastic filter tubes, I should like to hear about it.

I cannot, somehow, reconcile his statements with a mental picture of him scouring some twenty or thirty pounds of gravel until every particle of dust is removed. (The sand is then suitable for the fish to start fouling up again in a few days.) If lugging this disinfected gravel plus gallons of water drippingly to the waiting tank is not a task, I wonder what is. As for those children and invalids, I maintain that it borders on criminal negligence not to insist that their initiation into the fish fancy be contingent upon their having attendants with strong backs, steady nerves, and time to spend several hours daily in strenuous pursuit of their hobby.

In the three months since we were gulled into fish culture, I have spent considerable time indulging in such doubtless morbid speculation. It occupies my mind while I labor on behalf of our finny pets. It doesn't particularly enliven my leisure hours, but that is because I no longer have any. I never have much leisure in summer, when small Kay and her father, the Professor, both have nearly three months' vacation and our quarter-acre of lawn, shrubs, and gardens imposes its requirements upon the normal demands of the three of us, the house, and the cat. Add fish, and the life of a parkway policeman on Labor Day weekend seems pure holiday.

Our fish, like so many of the troubles that beset mankind,

came into our lives via a combination of innocence and good intentions. Kay had a long, serious illness in the late spring, shortly after her sixth birthday. Desperate for means to entertain her during almost a month in the hospital, we appealed for suggestions to everybody we knew. We were delighted when one of our friends offered to provide a small bowl of guppies for the bedside table. Something interesting for Kay to watch—colorful, inexpensive, no trouble at all!

Triumphantly, we bore the guppies and two little pond snails to Kay in the hospital, where they delighted her for about ten days. Then the fish died. We should have been warned, but we weren't. The cause of their deaths seemed so clear and avoidable: Repeated overfeeding had fouled the bowl until a well-meaning nurse tried to clean things up by changing the water. Tropical fish, unlike the more durable goldfish of my youth, can't stand fresh water. Their habitat has to be at least three days old in order to be safely purged of chlorine and other elements which otherwise prove fatal.

Kay pleaded eloquently for new fish upon her return home, so the Professor and I paid a visit to a tropical fish shop recently opened in our village. From then on we were gone geese.

THE BIRD IN THE BREAKFAST ROLL

Every once in a while, somebody in the Westchester village where we live brings up the subject of my church attendance or, rather, my lack of it. I always wonder what would happen if I told the simple truth: I really don't dare go.

The things that happen to me when I try, on Sunday mornings, to do my Christian duty form too long and intimidating a sequence for any sensible woman to ignore. And my convictions in the matter are not, I fear, such as to tempt me to buck my obvious fate.

Easter morning a couple of years ago, when the bird fell into the breakfast roll, put the lid on things but it was only the last act of a sorry drama that goes back as far as I can remember. Farther, in fact, for I have forgotten the mornings when mother kept me quiet during the sermon by providing pencils and paper. I have no recollection of the cat which mother says I "ruined" by coloring it blue, nor of the portrait I did, aged four, of our minister baptizing a baby. Recently, I heard with something of a shock that he kept that one; it turned up after his death, among papers in his private safe. I wonder what it could have been like.

I do remember, clearly, the time when I risked damnation at age seven or eight to sneak a swallow of "communion wine." It was Welch's grape juice, unadulterated by anything more potent than water. I felt strongly that the parson was lying from the pulpit when he called it anything else, but since I knew what would happen if I were to explain my reasons for thinking so, I kept my opinions to myself.

Perhaps they subconsiously colored my later views about the duplicity of much ecclesiastical ceremony. If so, they received considerable support in my early teens, when the church in the small country town where we lived recruited a choir from the local high school population. I, who am wholly tone deaf and cannot even growl on more than two notes, filled a stall in the front row of that choir for nearly two years, under strict orders to move my mouth in appropriate fashion but never, under any circumstances, to emit a sound. Every week, I dutifully practiced mouthing hymns inaudibly in front of our bathroom mirror, and to this day I feel that the demise of silent movies about that time deprived me of a chance at a wonderful career for which I had had invaluable basic training.

I slept on Sunday mornings, during college in the irreligious '30s. But toward the end of World War II, I was married in a church—or, at least, a chapel—and that ceremony, too, had its odd aspects.

The locale caused confusion because my fiancé was a naval officer and we were married at Fort Lincoln, Maryland, which sounds like an army post. Actually, it is a federal cemetery. We picked it for the simple reason that we thought the bridegroom was about to be shipped to Europe and a marriage license obtained in Maryland then required no waiting period for servicemen who provided their own chaplain and had the wedding performed on federal property.

We got our mothers to Washington somehow, rounded up a Navy chaplain who distinguished himself by keeping his eyes almost wholly shut throughout the proceedings, corralled some twenty or thirty friends, and did the deed in proper military fashion on D-Day plus 365.

My roommate went to town in the matter of bridal bouquets and photographs, with somewhat mixed results. I am not tall and I like my flowers, if any, as simple as possible. The dinner-plate-sized concoction of Talisman roses, freesias, and lilies of the valley that I was forced to clutch made me feel exactly like the Queen of a Firemen's Carnival. I am told that I juggled it from hand to hand as I went to claim my bridegroom.

That does not surprise me; what does surprise me is that I got there at all. The resident custodian or sexton, whatever his title was, helpfully volunteered to conduct me around the outside of the building to a side door where somebody had decided I should enter. After a fifteen-minute tour of vestibules, corridors, passageways, and one unmistakable potting shed, he landed me in a small, rectangular grass plot completely surrounded by a three-foot boxwood hedge. There was no break anywhere in the hedge except the one by which we had entered, although the desired door was finally visible some distance away.

Fortunately, I was married wearing a suit and wartime skirts where short. I leaped the hedge and made it for the ceremony, trying hard to conceal unbecoming hilarity.

Immediately afterward, the excellent, imported photographer lost either his wits or his vision and took a portrait shot of bride and groom in front of the altar with the cross sprouting neatly from dead center of my flowered hat. His other pictures were satisfactory, but I still start when that one turns up among the others in the family archives.

We had no further eccesiastical experiences until after our daughter was born, when her paternal grandmother became concerned about my heathen influence. She was tactful about it, but persistent. Things came to a head during the summer when New York State employed Dr. Howell, the rain-maker. Grandma did not share our amusement over the row that our four-year-old had with a contemporary: Its cause was, according to our Kay, that "Suzie kept saying God makes it rain and any fool knows it's Dr. Howell!"

Thereafter, to keep peace in the family, we enrolled our offspring in Sunday School. Sunday mornings, hitherto peaceful affairs, promptly assumed the hellish aspect of all those other mornings when people had to follow schedules requiring urgency, organization, and chauffeuring. They also, for some reason which I have never been able to figure out, led us into a long series of involvements with assorted livestock.

There was the time when we were awakened about 6 a.m. by screams from the study. Our cat Beer, we found, had let himself out his private cat door, caught a baby rabbit, and hauled it upstairs by the ears for disposal in a literary atmosphere.

It died of fright before we even managed fairly to rescue it and Kay had to be forcibly restrained from dressing up the corpse for use as a doll. That Sunday began with an unceremonial burial.

There was also the time when my husband, now a civilian university professor, roused us from sleep with a yell from the back window: "Come quick! There's the biggest rat I ever saw out under the maple tree!"

It wasn't a rat; it was an opossum en route to the woods at the foot of our street from a neighbor's chicken house. Not only is an opossum no object to contemplate intimately the first thing in the morning, but this one's recent diet apparently had been ill advised: The mess it deposited in mid-lawn engendered no proper Sunday emotions in us when we had to swab it up.

There were more episodes than I care to remember involving Beer, mice, moles, and an occasional bird. Even in his youth, Mr. B. was no hunter, thank goodness; nowadays, I think a bird would have to fly into his waiting jaws before he would deign to notice it. But almost all his forays upon local small game took place on Sunday mornings during those years of Kay's religious education.

I shall pass lightly over the day when he brought a full-grown blue jay, quite unhurt, into our bedroom and released it in my sleeping face. It pecked the Professor severely before he succeeded in driving it out the window.

I should prefer to forget the occasion upon which Beer brought in a mouse, then lost it under the kitchen stove where, we discovered, a strategic bit of floor molding was missing. The mouse fled into the wall, while the Professor commented bitterly upon the situation. The gist of his remarks, repeated at intervals throughout the day, was that most people presumably kept cats in the hope that they would rid a place of mice, while we, apparently, kept a cat so that he might stock the joint with them. (The mouse eluded Beer, but I got it subsequently in a trap baited with bacon rind.)

Beer provided the penultimate episode in our Sunday morning sequence one rainy 8 o'clock before anybody had had coffee, as usual. The Professor went out in the drizzle and came charging back to greet me at the kitchen door:

"Beer is out by the purple cane raspberries eating something that looks like a human fetus!"

The astounding fortitude of most wives and mothers is a matter of record. Still, I marvel slightly to recall that, of all the ways in which I might have met this announcement, I merely said, "Oh?", and went out to investigate.

The "human fetus" turned out to be small, repulsive, pink, and semi-transparent. Nauseatingly close inspection of the shape of its head led me to conclude that it was a very young opossum, lost out of mamma's pouch on one of her trips to the chicken house. Beer indicated strongly that he wished to retain possession of it, so I left him in command of the field, for once shutting the cat door against him. (I don't think I could have coped with the situation indoors, at that hour.) He apparently ate the creature, with no ill effects. At least, we couldn't find a trace of it when we searched the yard after the Sunday School run, and Beer continued healthy.

After that came the Easter payoff. Special church occasions always caused confusion in our house, because on such days Sunday School was sometimes held, sometimes cancelled. I never did manage to grasp what rule applied when, so that Christmas, Easter, etc. were regularly marked by recriminations, hasty breakfasts, and painful deferment of the Sunday *Times*.

This particular Easter was rendered especially awkward by

my hitherto irreproachable mother-in-law's sudden resort to bribery. She sent us an Easter check with orders to use it to buy the best dinner available on condition that we all went to church first!

The Professor and his daughter seemed to find nothing odd in this. My first reaction was sheer fury. Then I backed away from the inevitable row, rationalizing my feeble surrender by deciding that it wasn't worth hurting grandma's feelings over and besides, better people than I had sold out for less. Who was I to turn up my nose at Manero's steak?

Then I had one of those lapses of memory that had fouled us up before. I was sure Sunday School didn't keep on Easter, so we got up about 9 to a morning geared for 11 o'clock church. Kay immediately plunged us into chaos by proclaiming that there was 9:30 Sunday School. Each child was to receive a begonia (or a geranium, or something of the sort) and she wasn't going to be cheated out of hers.

A hasty phone call proved her right about the hour, no offer to buy her a dozen assorted plants next day had any effect, and I found myself, in bathrobe and slippers, frantically coping with orange juice while the Professor and his daughter dressed.

When I let Beer out for his morning stroll (he has to eat on the first shift or you can't move in the kitchen without stepping on him), I noticed an unfamiliar object lying on the lawn beside the bird bath. It looked like a discarded black glove, as much as anything. Neither Beer nor I gave it another thought until Kay hit the kitchen, shrieking that it was a disabled bird, and Beer would kill it.

"Bird, nothing," I snorted. "Looks as if one of the kids who lose baseballs over our fence got mad and heaved his glove over after it."

Kay, in slip and socks, insisted hysterically that it was a bird in mortal danger and that I must rush to the rescue. She managed, in the excitement, to knock over both her milk and her orange juice. Just then the wretched object wiggled feebly, right on cue. I loathe rushing about the yard in a bathrobe, but I had no choice. The "glove," on closer inspection, turned out to be a redwing blackbird with no visible signs of injury other than a tendency to act as if he'd been hit on the head.

Later, I found out that he had been: A neighbor had seen him fly head-on into a grape arbor, fall down stunned for a minute, then flap dizzily off. Now we had inherited him, in an advanced stage of concussion.

I dislike handling birds. It is probably unfeminine of me, but I find birds much more unpleasant to touch than snakes. The latter are chilly in the hand, as you expect, while birds' reptilian claws are shockingly hot. Distastefully, I marched back indoors with the invalid, put him in a handy grocery carton where he lay inert while Kay crooned over him, and mopped up what appeared to be about a gallon of mixed milk and orange juice.

I was trying to parry our daughter's questions as to what was to be done with the bird, partly because I didn't have any answers handy and partly because I hate any conversation at all prior to coffee, when the Professor arrived on the scene. Going out to reconnoiter, he made a discovery that I had overlooked.

"Some cat has been sick at the foot of the steps," said the Professor, cheerfully, "You'll have to do something about it, darling".

Muttering language highly inappropriate to Easter morning, I went out again in that inconvenient bathrobe and cleaned up the mess.

When I finally waved father and daughter on their way, I thought at last I'd be able to have the coffee I had been wanting for what seemed like a long, long day. I was just lifting the pot off the stove when all hell broke loose behind me: swish-flutter-CRASH-bang-squawk-flip-flap-flop!

Our bird, it appeared, had come to. Whether warmth or the smell of coffee revived him, I do not know. What I do know is that he took off with his throttle wide open, zoomed straight up in the air without looking, hit the ceiling at full speed, and knocked himself out again. He lay, kicking feebly, flat on his back in the exact middle of a breakfast roll that was resting hospitably on the kitchen table. Aimlessly waving wings knocked pieces of pecan and raisins hither and yon.

Setting my teeth hard, I fished him out and dusted him off. He was full of sugar frosting; the breakfast roll was well larded with bits of black feathers. I put an old window screen over the top of the carton this time and consigned the remains of the breakfast roll to the garbage can. When the Professor got home after delivering his daughter, I had just achieved coffee.

We had some sort of breakfast, after which scrabblings in the grocery carton heralded the bird's return to consciousness. The Professor took him down to the woods and turned him loose, returning to report that he took off like a bat out of hell on an unswerving course that apparently missed all visible trees. Whether he continued to miss them or not, I neither know or care. My daughter later upbraided me for abandoning him, but he flew out of our lives, which was all that seemed to matter at the moment.

We were somewhat late for church. However, we got there. The only thing I remember about the service is that the minister, an excellent speaker and writer, mispronounced a word during the sermon and my learned nine-year-old called my attention to the fact in a clarion stage whisper.

Dinner at Manero's was excellent. Knowing that grandma would have disapproved use of her money for the purpose, I anted up enough of my own for two double martinis before I had the strength to tackle it.

Our daughter dropped out of Sunday School the next fall. Nowadays, I drink my coffee peacefully on Sunday mornings, read the papers, and let the day develop as it will. I'm getting too old to tangle with things ecclesiastical any more. I just don't have the nerve.

[28 *November 1951*]

I don't know why, after months of mental inactivity, I suddenly feel thoughtful . . . and journal-ish. Approaching winter has something to do with it, I suppose. This has been such a glorious fall—after a wholly inadequate summer that drowned us in chilly rain almost all the time, except for spasms of steaming heat—that one has for weeks been content simply to revel in weather. I can't remember another year when I loved fall best of the seasons. But this one was better than spring . . . blue, clear, hot in the sun, with bracing winds. Not threatening winter and chill and death at all. Rather, holding glad carnival, after which all nature would turn happily to sleep for a while.

So one contemplates winter without qualms. Wonderful October extending unprecedentedly into November—November here is usually such a horrid month—has left me in a mood to enjoy mental processes and purr before the fire. If we had one!

I *wish* we had a fire. Before another winter, I have sworn, I'm going to find us a house of space, inside and out, and fireplaces.

It will take some finding. Can one, possibly, locate anything like an honest farmhouse with a few acres of privacy within commuting distance of New York? Even remotest commuting distance? We wouldn't want an estate even if we could afford it. And real estate agents hereabouts seem to find no happy medium between estates and dry-goods-boxes.

At present, we're living in a pretty good example of the dry-goods-box category. It has become dear to us, over four years, because we've been through so much together. In our early days it presented us with most of the crises that a house can think up to smite you with, and we got through them, somehow. Leaky roofs and leaky basements, falling plaster and recurrent explosions of archaic plumbing, cranky doors and windows, flaking paint and chipping putty—we had them all. We also had, for six initial desperate weeks, a pot stove. To anyone who has ever been similarly afflicted, I need say no more. To anyone who, like me when I first contemplated it, is forced to inquire of a convenient workman, "What on earth is that thing?", it requires explanation.

Briefly, our pot stove was a fat iron affair about twice the size of the average scrub bucket, sitting in the cellar around the corner from the furnace and connected—somewhat dubiously, it turned out—to the same chimney. Supposedly, you stoked it liberally with chestnut coal two or three times a day, whereupon by means of conglomeration of elderly pipes, it imparted heat to a totally inadequate twenty-gallon hot water tank on the other side of the chimney.

Actually, by dint of ten times that many sessions of filling, shaking down, and general hand holding, it produced about two feeble tankfuls daily. My daughter being still in diapers, my newly acquired Bendix and I found hot water for the laundry a problem.

The stove itself was also a problem. It probably would have burned us up the first night after we moved in if I hadn't happened to bump that dubious chimney connection. Our plumber, one of the kindest of men and my constant adviser during those early days (Hillier was in Europe, that first month, so I had the settling-in job alone!) was explaining to me the pot stove's operation. Bending down to look into its funny round maw, I braced myself against the pipe—and my hand went clean through it! Startled, we examined rusty pipe remains that turned out to be about the consistency of tissue paper. The whole thing crumbled in our hands.

Mr. McGuire was equal to that emergency. In an hour or so, we had a shiny elbow of new pipe in the offending spot. But nobody could do anything about the insides of that execrable stove. The previous owners of our house did the most peculiar things to their lares and penates, apparently in the name of makeshift repairs. In this case, they had sawed off the end of the grates, so that no known shaker would fit snugly enough to make the necessary half-turn.

That first evening, Mr. McGuire did it with a Stillson wrench. Thereafter, being unwilling to invest in expensive tools for the sake of a "heating system" which was going out of our lives as fast as I could buy replacements, I evolved a system. If you hooked the end of a rusty old shaker I found in the coal bin to the bit of grate that protruded, braced it inboard toward the stove with all your strength, and then hammered down viciously on it, it worked! The noise it made in that gloomy basement at midnight (if I didn't sit up 'til then, the stove went out and we had no warm water in the morning) was enough to rouse the neighborhood. Also, I developed a kink in my right shoulder that lasted several months.

I am infuriatingly right-handed. My left is no good for anything. Its inability to wield a hammer forced me, already prayerfully down upon one knee, to brace the shaker with my left hand, clutch the hammer in my good right fist, twist myself about in a ballerina attitude, and hammer away from my body across that braced left arm. As an exercise for beneficially stretching the waist muscles, that probably was a honey. As a performance that had to be gone through ten or a dozen times a day in order to obtain the flow of tepid water out of our rusty taps, it ranked near the top of my list of annoyances. It took such a lot of time, too. And time, in those days, was something I rationed with miserly precision.

Somebody finally diagnosed my pot stove's insatiable appetite as a case of more amateur tinkering. The grates had been raised. I imagine the previous owners sawed them off too short and had to shove one side up out of the stove's fat belly to its narrower neck to compensate. So, of course, the firebox was proportionately smaller and wouldn't hold enough coal at one time to last for more than three or four hours. Also, it burned in an odd, lopsided fashion that necessitated constant poking to reallocate coals.

Altogether, that stove was one of my major tribulations; it reduced me to a state of such fury that I sold it to a scrap-iron dealer for fifty cents, a week after our current heating system was installed. Now, in retrospect, I rather regret that rash act. It was a cunning little fat stove, for all its shortcomings. I wonder if we shouldn't have kept it to plant herbs in, or otherwise use about the place as a conversation piece? But at the time, I wanted only to banish it from my ken forever. With the memory of those midnight hammerings still reverberating in my ears, I can understand why.

[28 November . . . evening]

Our poor Kay continues to brush up against society's limiting frustrations at a great rate. I do not know . . . I do not know about Barry Avenue kindergarten. Since I am not at all "up" on educational theory, I find myself infuriatingly unable to argue the point. Anybody who is, or poses as, an expert can flatten me. However tangled up in words I may get, however, I believe unshakably that the aim of education is to rouse curiosity, to stimulate, to excite young minds, to offer, delicately, new ideas and see what the customer makes of them. To start him on the way to developing ideas of his own. To thrill him with the great ones his forerunners have had. Ideally . . . and idealistically . . . to stimulate, with a dash of pragmatism thrown in as a leaven. And above all, damn it, in this too regimented, too collectivized world we live in, to apply that general theory to individuals with an eye to their individualities. You can't start that too young. And you mustn't ever stop.

I suppose it's all very well to cry "an end to assembly line techniques!" when you don't have to try to find alternatives. And I realize these teachers of Kay's are up against an almost insurmountable problem with their one old room, vintage about 1870, and their thirty-seven five-year-olds crammed into it. Physical fact probably forces them to regiment somewhat. But can't it be done in such a way that any perceptive one among the little victims may realize it isn't the ideal, or even the proper, way?

Kay seems to think that she's under compulsion to try to be like everybody else . . . as if all children, or most, don't want to conform to a degree highly alarming, at least to me. All do the same thing at the same time, not because we're sorry but there isn't room to do otherwise, but because, QED, that is what we do. And she must find it odd to be treated as an infant, when at home and at the good nursery school where she formerly went, she has always been treated like a reasonable human being. A young human being, subject to the restraints and limitations adherent thereto. But nevertheless, a thinking person.

I blew up first over the painting situation. Only to Hillier, poor lamb. I can't get the Rye Neck Board of Education to purchase adequate supplies if it won't or can't, and it would do no good for me to tackle a teacher's methods when supplies aren't available to permit better methods. But Kay, our Kay who loves to paint, and who has been doing some things with water colors and long brushes that appear not only to her fond parents but to other observers to show a nice feeling for color and form, came home shortly after school started this fall to report the following:

She can't get a chance to paint very often because she isn't "quiet enough." Probing to find out what in the world that meant, I discovered that painting, with two double-sided easels available for thirty-seven kids, is employed as a reward for virtuous deportment.

"When we come in," she said, "we go and sit in our seats with our hands folded. We have to be very quiet, Mummy.

And then the teachers look around and they pick the four quietest ones and tell them they can paint, and then they ask the rest of us what we want to do."

"What *do* you want to do?" I asked her.

"If I can't paint, I'd rather color," said she. "I almost always color. Sometimes we play with the blocks, or in the doll corner, but mostly I color."

We primed her so hard to go ask for a turn painting that shortly thereafter she got one. I do not know how quiet our active, intent daughter managed to be. Subsequently she brought home an insipid looking pastel effort for approval. I tried to approve, but I must have sounded lukewarm because she hastened to explain:

"It would be better if we could mix the colors, but we have to use just the ones they give us." (In this case, pale blue, pale pink, and a sort of faded wheat color.)

I said, "But you know enough to mix colors in a separate dish and clean brushes before you put different colors on them!"

She does. But the rule is the rule. Some children undoubtedly would make a mess and, anyhow, I guess it's too much trouble!

Why must the end product of mass anything—education, social and economic equalities, arts, or crafts—be to level down?

Today she started singing while we shelled almonds for the Christmas cookies, stopped suddenly, and inquired if I minded. When I stared in horror she giggled and told me she knew I didn't, but Miss MacDonald did. You mustn't sing at school except at singing time because it might interfere with the person near you who is concentrating on something.

Granted you can't have thirty-seven children all singing different songs at the tops of their lungs, this is a *kindergarten*, not a senior high school. Can't they hum, softly, to themselves? Or have more "singing time" . . . there isn't a lot?

No parent should undercut pedagogical authority, even when it's being used all wrong. Still, I can't subscribe to these things utterly. I told her that of course, at school, she must do as Miss MacDonald tells her, though I, personally, didn't know whether I'd tell her that if I were the teacher, and to remember, please, that at home she can sing every blessed minute if she wants to and I'll love to hear her. I do.

"Every day," said she with a small grin. "Miss MacDonald says,'What is that noise? Is somebody singing?' And then she tells me to stop. Every day it's me!"

I *will not* tell her that in that case she'd better remember not to sing; let the teachers do that if they must . . . in a kindergarten! And at home, she shall have music.

[29 November 1951]

A glorious day, blue and gold with melted frost making muddy patches in the gardens. Wild thyme on the front bank, still valiantly unfrozen, has poked its little green tips as far as possible above sheltering leaves toward its love, the sun. The old gray rocks that bolster its steeply sloping bed are warm to the touch. And O, the smell of thyme in sunshine, in almost-December.

These autumnal surprises, similar unseasonal gallantries in winter thaws and earliest spring, are among the great joys of herb gardeners. I love my herbs for their doughtiness. Long after the showy flowers my neighbors cherish have gone with the black frosts, the herb garden greets us with fragrant foliage shaded in exquisite greens and grays. Sometimes it even produces brave bits of blossom in latest fall.

This very mild season, we are particularly garden-rich. Wild marjoram is waving woolly gray-green leaves above darker green thyme on the bank; lemon thyme mingles its green-gold with its darker relatives in the back rock garden; hyssop, always last of all to succumb to winter here, is flourishing in dark shrubby clumps. In the sunny side bed, my lavender has barely felt the hoar frosts of recent November nights. Its delicate blue-gray . . . almost a rosy gray in places . . . contrasts exquisitely with hyssop behind it.

There is one amusing aspect to that lavender bed. When

weeds back of the clothes lines are gone and shrubs have lost their protective screen of leaves, the cats shift their daily games to the lavender and hyssop gardens. Muffling foliage is essential to feline mock battlefields. Beer, with his glossy black and white—he positively gleams in the sun, these days—sticks out arrantly against landscape. But his neighbor and chum, Puff, blends almost invisibly into the gray-green-blue of lavender. I hadn't realized how much blue there was in Puff's soft gray coat until one day last fall, when I finally had to drop kitchen chores and go investigate whatever it was that Beer was scrooching at so madly outside my window. I was within three feet of him before I distinguished Puff among surrounding plants. (I often think what a pity it is that the Varleys, with whom he lives, are not herb gardeners. If they were, how nice it would be for them to have a cat that matched a lavender bed!)

Beyond the lavender, germander is still a low-growing clump of darkest green-blue, with silver lace behind it—artemisia frigida, like a three-dimensional version of frost-etchings on a winter windowpane. It is as soft as it looks, too, when you brush fingers against it.

Basils and marjoram have succumbed to frost, of course. Lemon balm, spotted monarda, and the bergamots present only tiny, stunted leaves still trying to grow cuddled close to the ground. I have cut back my tarragon for the winter. Beyond it, that widespeading, sturdy perennial that was given to me as "English primrose"—which it almost certainly isn't—is represented only by reddish rosettes of leaves, flat against chilly soil. More than a dozen little red rosettes around each parent stem, the obliging thing's children, almost crowd us out of garden space annually. But in June we can't get enough of their buttercup-yellow blossoms with funny little four-pronged stars on their tips. They are breathtaking against tall, deep blue anchusa.

I have spent hours trying to identify that yellow plant. Garden books invariably decline to provide illustration. Finally, in a seed catalogue, I came across a list of forms of "oenothera, the sundrop," and I am almost sure that one of them must be our beloved blaze of yellow. I have decided that its unpronounceable botanical name really doesn't matter anyway. Unless by some awful chance it stops flourishing for us, so that I have to go out searching for it among nurserymen—we couldn't imagine the garden without it—all I need to know is that it's our Mary Jane primrose, and we love it.

The great mulleins that wandered into the north border this year still defy November with fat clumps of woolly pale green. Everybody assures me mullein is an awful weed that should be banished violently from beds and borders. It is a proud old herb, though; I'm glad it came to live with us. Those fat leaves, almost a quarter of an inch thick, delight me. Thick and soft as the blankets we used to tuck on Kay's crib, they are. No wonder mullein can withstand November. It should be able to withstand any cold, clad as it is in woolens—but I suppose it won't.

In a sunny front corner of that same hardy border, nepeta mussini continues to poke little sprigs of gray-green above leaf mulch. The cats probe hopefully every day in its vicinity, gleefully discovering tender sprigs to delight their palates. They also roll in it, especially Puff. Beer does not permit his lazy dignity more than a whisker rub against his favorite tonic, but Puff, always more energetic, charges in with the energy of a small child attending a pillow fight. He thrashes about, wallowing ecstatically, grazes to his heart's content then—flop!—down he goes into that inviting gray-green mattress and simply grovels. Which is one reason my nepeta lives against a background of durable, woody plants. Some infant French thyme that I once installed in its vicinity suffered considerably from Puff's enthusiasm.

Further along our borders, grays seem to predominate. Santolina stretches arms like delicately cut gray coral above a huddle of brown ash and maple leaves at is base. (Those leaves should all be removed. It is much too early for mulches; I find it is usually better not to mulch anyway here in the

Sound country. Wait until the earth freezes fast in December, spread oak leaves and salt hay with loving care, and Nature promptly becomes soft and soggy. The poor overdressed plants rot in their muddy wet covering.)

Another gray that I love is horehound. I like its bitter taste, too. Tea with a medicinal tang—but such pleasant medicine. Also the woods-tasting hard candies of my youth. Nobody else in the family can bear the flavor of it, though they applaud round, hairy leaves whose gray is almost blue. I have only one objection to it; seeds with an aggressively burr-like composition which I must remember to cut out relentlessly before they get a chance to ripen. If I forget, my poor Beer comes in from garden strolls with his long coat miserably matted. They tangle especially in his soft white shirt-front and his fluffy underpinning. Then we have melodrama getting them out. Beer loathes having his pants combed.

At the far end of the north border, where pale pink bee-balm and blue spires of anise-hyssop rioted last summer, fat clumps of spicy pinks tilt little gray spears against approaching December. Their gray is the most blue of all.

Mints have been cut back, but sturdy bits remain fresh as they were in September. Peppermint has hairy, dark green leaves ranged along the reddest of stems; next to it, spearmint's lighter green still is aromatic of iced tea and juleps; bergamot mint presents smooth reddish greens, while at the end of the row, apple mint contrasts a harlequinade of green and white. Apple mint, mixing its spring greens with white borders, splotches, and wavery stripes, is one of my favorites. This spring I found one wandering shoot that was pure white—almost eight inches long—mingling its soft paleness with its variegated neighbors. Exquisite on a warn gray boulder.

In the "vegetable garden," which gives up more vegetable space to herbs every year, hoary old sage has bowed its blue-gray head slightly in deference to frosts. But there are still fresh leaves in the heart of each bushy tip. I nibbled one this morning, then rushed in to get a bit of cheese to go with it.

Fresh sage leaves on cheese sandwiches are a palatal thrill.

Cucumber-flavored burnet continues to thrust delicate curls of new leaf, palest green, up among the blue of its old foliage. Beyond it, flat-leaved parsley is a thrifty, useful row—after Thanksgiving! But I have even gone to that garden in December and found edible bits of parsley and burnet. Once we unearthed them from a snow-drift.

Lovage, whose summer produce fills fat jars on the kitchen shelf, has finished its season. I always dry a lot of it. What would turkey stuffing be without tablespoonsful? Or, in lesser amounts, dressing for avocado salads, certain casserole dishes, and chicken pie? One of our favorites, lovage.

Queued along neatly beside the bare spot where fat hybrid tomatoes flourished, a double row of leeks presents tall green tops. Transplanting them laboriously, spear by spear, was a day's job last spring; later they repaid us with luscious bowls of vichyssoise, topped with the chives that now are almost gone. And these chilly days, our leeks provide, in combination with potatoes, milk, and paprika, a favorite winter soup now available without endless market searchings. I always wonder why leeks aren't more in demand.

Alpine strawberries that I started from seed (in a coffee tin) exhibit reddish-tipped leaves, still unfrozen. Those strawberries bore, this year, until late October!

Borage and summer savory are gone; garden cress and dill failed to survive the heavy frosts that ushered in Thanksgiving. On the bank beyond the raspberry bushes, our perennial blue flax droops somewhat. Thickly clustered at the base of each plant, branches like miniature, spiky evergreens will wither soon. Flax is one of our joys. From late June until October, every morning it is covered with new blossoms, delicately veined, heavenly blue. On sunny days the four flat petals drop by early afternoon, but when we are shrouded in fog or rain, they linger almost until evening.

Back in our woods corner, where the shrubs grow thick, myrtle leaves are glossy dark green among dead brown fern fronds. At the edge of the bed, where lilies of the valley and deep purple woods violets are benison in spring, ivy trails boldly still. Woodbine on the fence shivers, bare-stemmed. But in the front of the bed is our most spectacular herb triumph of all. Chervil flourishes there in deep maple shade where I was advised that nothing would grow. Chervil, most tempermental of our herbs, declined politely to live in any of half a dozen supposedly favorable spots where I cherished it with humus and painstaking care. It grew a few feeble inches, yellowed, and died. Finally, in despair I transplanted a batch of it—chervil is supposed to die immediately if disturbed!—to that sour, swampy bit of maple shade. It throve. The following spring its blossoms were fifteen inches tall; its foliage gave us a harvest for winter seasoning. And its self-sown progeny continue merrily to cover the same area. Protected by leaves and shrubbery, bits of chervil are miraculously green even now. I think I could find enough to flavor a green salad, or impart special delicate tang to a breakfast egg.

Later . . .

Writing about the herb garden with mid-afternoon sun flooding in the window beside me, I suddenly found it unbearable to stay indoors. I couldn't go beyond our quarter-acre because I had to wait for the Bendix man to come and diagnose the latest ailment of that dyspeptic machine, but at least I didn't have to sit in the house.

Outside, the gardens smelled of spring. Baking hot sun on earth that has been soaked in alternate frost and condensation from heavy fog produces odors of March mud. I love that smell.

Beer seems to love it, too, though he hates mud underfoot. Touring gardens with me, he bounced exuberantly into muddy spots which necessitated desperate sessions of foot-washing. Mud between the toe-pads, mud in the longish black and white fluff that cushions his claws, is no joke. He spreads his toes to their widest and frantically bites.

Spring in November stimulated him, nevertheless. Crouching and scuttering with many "prr-ups," he implored me to play his favorite game of tag. Obligingly, I pursued. To play his game properly, you wait while he scrooches, rush at him with mock ferocity, then chase while he races to a new starting point behind convenient cover. He usually makes a beeline for the ash tree early in the proceedings, to sharpen claws on his pet scratching post. (He and Puff both use that ash tree. They have carded wool on it so long and strenuously that it presents a queer spectacle. For more than two feet up its trunk, the bark is so shredded and furred that it looks like peat moss.)

After his bout with the ash tree, Mr. Beer felt need of more agile company than mine. His next rush carried him under the fence, where he goes when he no longer wants people to follow. Tail aloft, he pranced downhill in search of his fluffy friend.

His departure didn't leave me long alone, this time. I barely had time to pay my respects to the clary sage (which I forgot earlier, and shouldn't have because it is beautiful) when I heard small, snapping noises behind me. The black squirrel was sitting on the garden table not ten feet away, engrossed in a hickory nut. I can't believe he needed that nut particularly. All the squirrels are fat as butter this time of year, and our little friend, with his coat shading from black to chocolate brown with reddish tints, is one of the chunkiest. He has always been very tame. The other squirrels are horrid to him, probably because he is different from their unalloyed grayness. During the hickory nut season they would not tolerate him in the trees, chasing him fiercely out of orthodox preserves. He had to do his harvesting in the dead hours of the day, noon 'til the end of siesta time, when everybody else was home resting.

But his alarm at sight of alien squirrels does not extend to people. Maybe he uses up all his capacity for fear against quadrupeds. I wish he would develop a little more discretion. He wandered down the drive one day while I was going to get the car out, so near that I could almost have tweaked his tail.

Then when I started backing toward him, he refused to move. He actually sat there until I couldn't see him around the rear bumper, when I had to stop, get out, and chase him. I fear he won't find all motorists so considerate.

I do hope nothing happens to him. After he finished his nut this afternoon he sat politely, while I discussed the weather with him, without a shade of alarm on his little round face. In contrast to the rest of his coat, his muzzle is gunmetal gray. He must have inherited that nose-color from a parent, however; he isn't old. A last spring's baby.

Finally, leisurely, he uncurled himself from the sunny table top. His layers of fat show up more than ever when he balances in profile, on all fours. Good winter insurance, he has, against lean days ahead. I almost expected him to bounce as he leaped—a butterball of a squirrel.

[*13 February 1952*]

It *is* a relief to have a typewriter that goes where you want it to. Though I am going to try very hard to do right by it, and not look at keys, which probably will mean typos for awhile.

I've never bothered to learn the top row of the keyboard—not even the invaluable punctuation marks one uses constantly—and lately I've got in a bad habit of looking at fingers while they flounder around the keyboard. This time, I'm resolved to master the thing.

I have spent much of the day doing finger-exercises, to Kay's fascination and Beer's pronounced disgust. (He says it's bad enough to have this noise going on part of the time, and no lap available when a deserving fluffy person wishes to take a nap. But when the noise goes purposefully on into the night, and it's too cold and blowy outside for comfortable prowling—well, he's annoyed and many have been the tail-twitches in my direction to tell me so.)

Spring, which has been paying us a wonderful but quite unseasonable visit, has deserted us today. This morning was *cold*—20 above zero, with a cold wind blowing and the ground humped in fearful tussocks and frozen ridges after a week of being mud. (Those ridges are not going to do the lawns and gardens any good. These in-and-out winters we get here are hard on plants. They melt half-a-dozen times a winter, then heave up when they freeze so that the air gets at their poor roots. I'd like, just for a change, to have a garden in a more consistent climate! And be able to grow delphinium, which develops awful crown rot and refuses to survive wet winters in the Sound country.)

The early crocuses have been waiting.

[*17 January 1954*]

We are finally getting some winter. Snow, not much but some, has stayed with us since Thursday, and it's windy and cold. After a second storm Saturday, there actually was snow enough so Kay used her sled a bit.

I continue to boggle at what they call that activity around here: Not sliding, as we did, or coasting, as our more formal parents did, or sledding, as middle westerners do, but "sleigh-riding." And a sled, so help me, is a "sleigh"!

First time I heard that term was in the snowy winter of '47, and great confusion ensued when I enquired if people got these sleighs from one of the local riding stables, and what was the rental?

Just heard about a new second-grade teacher from Boston who came the same cropper when one of her young charges told he had spent the weekend "sleigh-riding." There wasn't enough snow, she said, and kindly stick closer to the truth in the future. So later she had to eat her words when hilarious older hands among the teachers checked her out on local idiom.

In desperation because it's so windy-cold, Beer has begun asking me to play with him, evenings. I drag ropes and roll balls for him, and he cavorts like a kitten. But the little stinker has discovered a lovely game that I wish he'd forget: He shoots the ball under the big gray chair, hauls himself round and round it, all claws clutching slipcover, then, when the ball really is out of reach, waits for me to tip up that chair with one hand and poke the ball out with the other. Chair weighs a good hundred pounds, and is unwieldy modern besides. But no matter where I start him, that's how Beer and the ball wind up every few minutes. I'm wondering who is exercising whom?

He and I just had our workout, and tomorrow is another day among the buzzsaws. Which are making life rather grim: Last Monday, work crews started taking down our woods for the Thruway. So from 8 to 4:10 or so, two men with electric saws spend about one hundred seconds destroying what took one hundred years to grow, while other men chop the debris into convenient lengths and burn it.

I never thought I could dislike wood smoke so. But it permeates everything, and it's our woods burning.

They are leaving a few trees this side of the brook, but all the other side is going. No more dog walks or woodland rambles with the kids; no more dogtooth violets, jack-in-the-pulpits, toothworts, dogwood, deep purple violets, sumac, and shadblow; no more birds and rabbits and little white-footed mice.

Floss [our neighbor] was bewailing birds' nests, going down. She's right; half our birds undoubtedly will move a mile or so over into Saxon Woods next spring. But what bothers me most, this bitter weather, is the squirrels' nests. And their storehouse trees. Where will the poor little critters go and what will they eat, with February and March, their leanest months, ahead of us?

Last year I hauled in the bird feeder in mid-March. Bugs were back early and birds were doing fine. But I started putting out sunflower seeds again for the poor slab-sided squirrels. Baby squirrels come early in April, and parents have to make do on what nuts they can find from last fall until the early berries and seeds come in.

Every big tree that road crew is felling has a squirrel's nest in it! With snow on the ground, temperatures ranging from 15 to 25, and high gales blowing from the north.

I think the crows are moving. Every morning when those infernal bees start buzzing the trees down, the crows circle and cry. Then they fly off toward Saxon Woods. Their tall pines are in the path of the roadbed. And they know it.

Wind was from the brook to us today, due north, and I wanted to move myself. The saws sounded as if they were in the kitchen; I could hear the crash of every tree that fell. And the smoke blew and blew by, and came in every time anyone opened a door.

The crew is offering wood to everybody who wants it, even chopping it into convenient lengths for carting away. So people with fireplaces are stocking up. But that's small comfort to anyone for losing the woods. The far side of the brook looks like a bombed-out area; stumps and ashes, and smoke that never quite stops even at night.

Beer is afraid of the saws! How can I tell him that interminable sound is not the growling of some terrible, large animal that eats small fat black-and-white cats alive?

He won't go out farther than an accommodation stop in the nearest garden, while they're working. Sits on the windowsill and stares and stares toward the brook, with enormous round scared eyes.

Almost he makes me superstitious. I feel so violently about this kind of "progress"—this idiot insane damned vandalism—that I wonder sometimes what he knows that we don't, and if this mess means bad cess to everybody?

One thing I know that those high-powered State engineers apparently don't: If the foreman who told Flossie and me, this morning, where they plan to start raising the road bed of their fine, streamlined six-lane highway knew what he was talking about, at least a quarter-mile of it is going to be under water several times a year! Because they are, he said, going to run level across the field-mouse meadow (now a waste land of

burned grass and sumacs). And the brook covers most of the meadow every twenty-four-hour rain; small boys take rowboats out on it.
 Well—may the trucks go swimming!!
 Beer and I have to go to bed.

[*23 February 1954*]

The rains have descended. Days of nasty, cold rain and fog—and fifty-seven varieties of sniffles prevalent all over town. So many third-graders are sick that I just got a call, "No hobbies this afternoon." Not enough kids on deck to make it worthwhile!

Our driveway is a duck pond, especially that low place where Beer and Puff once, jointly, went skating. Beer crosses in delicate, disdainful bounds. Even so, the "feathers" between his toes pick up spectacular amounts of mud to be deposited all over the house. How I dread the mud season! Now to be with us, bar an occasional freeze-up, for a couple of months, I suppose.

The first snowdrops are out, bless them. And alpine crocuses have fat, promising-looking buds. They are late this year. Usually they make it before Washington's Birthday. A few times they've been out for Lincoln's, and once we even had blossoms in January. I suppose recent zero weather delayed them. Hope we're through with zero for this year. Snow wouldn't be so bad, but spring has been in the air for a week or so and zero would be discouraging.

Saturday, just at dusk, we were walking up the hill and heard much squawking and honking overhead: the Canada geese who nest around the reservoir, about twenty of them in formation, going it like mad to get home before dark. Hillier and Kay had never seen them travelling before. I did, once when we'd just moved here, an even bigger flock. They are early this year. May they be right about imminent spring! I wonder what the mallards who have always nested up our brook will think when they try to go home. All the islands have been dredged out and the swamps are to be drained and filled for the Thruway. A sickening mess. They are changing the brook's channel, running it from the wall at the foot of Bradley Street through our meadow, so we lose that, too. Nobody knew it was to go.

If warm weather holds and things clear a bit, I'm going to try to transplant some more of the bayberry that grows in the meadow. Years ago we moved a bit of it (feeling very guilty because we were looting county property) and we love it. Now that the meadow is to be bulldozed, I have no compunctions about taking all I can dig.

Saturday, just before the rains began, we walked across West Street up into Harrison through the wonderful, wild country where the bridle paths run. More than ever, I wonder at the thinking—if you can call it that—which engineered this Thruway route. Trees are down now, so you can follow the route: for a mile or so through solid swamp where cattails flourish, six feet tall; through three lakes whose depth I don't know, and then blasted across a rock ridge a good forty feet up!

Don't ask me how they propose to drain the swamp and the lakes. Or what will be done about the runoff from the two ridges that flank the valley.

Apparently marked for blasting are two ruins we shall miss. They must have been from a stone farmhouse built before the Revolution—two little stone foundations with parts of walls still standing, backed against the granite outcrop. The land must have been farmed for some time, because stretches of old stone wall remain fairly intact.

But not for long, I'm afraid. There was a clump of alder, growing inside the foundations of the little house, that we used to visit every spring: Walls sheltered it so that it flaunted yellow catkins weeks before alder buds burst in the open. And it has been cut down. So the little stone ruins are marked to go—along with the cattails and pussy willows, the red-wing blackbirds, and the muskrats. For whom there is no sanctuary left.

Friday, while we watched, the lumbering crew brought down a huge black oak with a hollow limb that had a squirrel in it! Nobody knew he was there until the tree hit the ground. He must have cowered inside his home while that screaming electric saw cut through his tree. He climbed out, dazed, then took off, slowly at first, then faster, into a Bradley Street backyard. Poor little refugee.

The tree men are through, over here. Bulldozing and dredging are beginning. Huge piles of drain pipe litter the place where the white pine grove was—there isn't a tree left. I wonder what will happen down by our station when this operation is done. All the swamps are to be drained and filled; every tributary rivulet that empties into our Mamaroneck River is to be piped; the channel is to be made almost straight down, banked high to keep the Thruway dry. Lord knows how much water those swamps absorbed; I don't. But I don't see how the river can fail to go down to Columbus Park like a millrace, and when it meets the Sheldrake River there, the Sheldrake will back up halfway to Larchmont!

That has almost happened, before. Things have improved since the Village dug a basin in Columbus Park, but the basin can't begin to hold what will hit it—the first real flood after the Thruway men get done. And the conduit under Halstead Avenue isn't big enough, either. It looks as though all the new industry our mayor is so proud of having inveigled into this town (which is not and shouldn't be industrial) will go swimming!

I can't weep for that, but people in that whole end of town will suffer. It's a nasty prospect.

[*1 September 1956*]

Labor Day weekend—and hotter than Fourth of July. Of course, it often is; yet one can't help feeling it shouldn't be. Particularly when there has been a glorious spell of fall the week before.

If one can look at these as merely "dog days" and forget those crisp blue mornings, the present is more bearable. But still not pleasant. Reading Nan Fairbrother (*An English Year*), I was struck by one place where we most definitely disagree. Struck, because we seldom do. But she explains her liking for June as a liking for the time of year comparable to one's own age, and wonders if people do not prefer their own time of the seasons.

I'd say, no. Children are more rapturous about winter (always presupposing "winter with snow"), or summer with its beaches, than early spring. The old dread the winter and turn all their being on spring as a focus of hope.

My months are more July or August than Miss Fairbrother's June, and midsummer seems to me the deadest time of all the year—worse than February's barren ice and gray, which at least has the virtue of cutting down to essentials, with its challenge of cold and simplicity of stark, clean line. Winter may have run long, but still we find winter etchings clear in the landscape. I prefer color to etchings, but color where I can see through to the essential line. Now nothing is clear. Spring greens are gone; deeper shades are bogged down in great lush clumps and clusters and tangles. Browning tips on four-foot weed stalks come as a positive, physical relief from all this semitropical abundance. Birds are, in the main, silent. Days stridulate with the rasp of cicadas, even through the hottest hours. And at night the crickets, later to provide exquisite autumn choruses, compete with hordes of katydids like a thousand small buzzsaws.

Heat holds one half-insensate; humidity fogs the brain until one feels smothered between featherbeds, trying to clear inner vision from encroaching quarts of half-melted marshmallows. One finds oneself silently screaming, "Come on, fall, give us frost!" Something has to give.

I am trying to remember if I have always felt this way. I think I didn't when I was my own woman, nobody's wife and mother, tied to a job of course but free sixteen of the twenty-four hours to do as I chose. When you could choose to go hungry if cooking dinner was too much trouble; when laundry could be kept to a minimum (and most of it farmed out); when no house and yard presented themselves in silent reproach if I elected to spend a weekend reading, or writing—or simply staring at the ceiling when heat stultified me.

Midsummer was recreation, then. But at my own midsummer, it is reluctant work and an unpleasant feeling of lack. Lack of what? Promise in the air? Challenge? I'm not sure.

But I look at these almost rank gardens, and wish I didn't have to wait to shift this plant that proved too tall for its appointed spot, or that one that is being crowded by a too-rampant neighbor. Of course, I get the clippers and prune the offending neighbor, but it's not the same as spring, when everything is a shifting pattern, or fall, when once again one remakes.

Perhaps this is proof that spring is the greater of the two change-seasons, spring and fall. For winter passes easily, on the whole. Enough struggle with the elements to give one a sense of conquering something, and always spring at the back of your eye. While in summer, one knows that the fall effort will merely be to get the gardens ready for sleep.

If you're very tired (and you often are with young), there is tremendous satisfaction in getting the baby ready for bed—but nothing to compare with the fun of getting her up to see what is new that she can show you in the new day.

Am I still the early side of midsummer, at almost forty?

And yet I'm sure it was Lewis Gannett, in *Cream Hill*, who called (and he was then older than I) July and August "the dead months." Of all the twelve.

One thing I'm sure of: Autumn is coming to the fore again, for me. As a child, in my early teens in Woodstock, I loved it best of all. "October's bright blue weather—"

Then through my twenties and early thirties, it held an unbearable sadness. A pervasive, soft nostalgia that had a way of sharpening suddenly to catch me by the throat like a knife-thrust.

But now again I love it, almost best. Who was it who said "autumn is so much richer than spring"? And the challenge is there: Take this beauty, and then face winter, and don't let it down you. Then, then you may have spring again.

Anticipation being almost always pleasurable beyond actuality, promise of spring in autumn surpasses spring itself.

Or is it only that spring leads inevitably to summer, and I'll take winter, any time from June 'til, in this climate, mid-September or early October?

Or is all this a fine case of self-delusion in early middle age?

Beer has been suggesting for some time that it is proper for me to stop making these noises on this machine and accompany him to bed. He nudges me gently, bows hopefully toward the stairs. Heat has him enchained, too. He is tactful, whereas in cooler nights he would set claws fervently in my ankle. He has stretched out on his rug under the coffee table, but I know he'd greatly prefer his throw at the foot of my bed. What clawings could not accomplish, the sight of that uncomfortable lump of black and white wool has: I shall stop these unprofitable speculations and offer him convoy upstairs.

[*19 August 1957*]

MEMO TO MYSELF

Item 1. on the list of things to remember:
That one of the greatest arts people should cultivate is to look on the positive side of things; to concentrate on the joy of living instead of the difficulties; to keep the happy moments and wash the others out.
AND to do it without being a damned Pollyanna!
Sometimes I wonder if, so far, I haven't done a better job teaching Boo [family name for our daughter] this than I have doing it myself. (How many things is this true of?)
F'rinstance:
How much time have I spent mourning the woods the Thruway devastated? Or swearing about the Thruway, about which, after all, I cannot do one solitary damned thing?
It's permissible to mourn one's dead. Grief for our lost green oasis is, I think, permitted me: but not to let too much time be consumed in it. Futility consumes so much of our time!
Many of our birds are still with us. In fact, the chickadees have moved up this way since their pine grove went. (So, of course—and damn it—have the crows; also the grackles

whose eyrie by the ex-dump is now cloverleaf under construction. But we haven't lost our songbirds yet.)

We have more squirrels than ever. I know, O my gardening friends, that they are often destructive to your lawns and flower beds. They damage mine, too. But *how* I'd miss them. Little varmints barrelling bravely through the snow; flirting their tails from maple branches; clasping paws touchingly over their hearts while they decide what sort of designs, if any, I have on them; babies using our hammock as a play ground, and the lovely pairs I have seen, making a ceremonial dance of their mating—waltzing to slow music. (A revelation of animals' delight in each other, that was. Dogs and cats, for example, make such heavy weather of their courtings. You wonder if they possibly can enjoy them. But there was no question about my squirrels.)

The rabbits may wreak havoc in the herbaceous borders. They do. But aren't they fun, hopping home through the back yards at daybreak?

Having owned pet white mice, years ago, I'm acquainted with the multifold fecundity of the rodent population. I'm grateful that I acquired this biological data: Otherwise, I'd find it hard to bear when Beer catches a wood mouse. Inept hunter that he is (thank goodness), he does bag one occasionally. And they are so soft and beautiful, so sweet and, before Beer pins them with a fluffy silver paw (which must look like an armored tank to them!), so gently preoccupied with their little mouse business.

There was the baby he brought in, of all times, during Thanksgiving dinner three years ago. It trembled in my hand, but it was not injured. I found a new cause for thankfulness when I took it out to run back into a crack of the stone wall. (And Beer found turkey tidbits a highly acceptable substitute!)

I have never heard a wood mouse sing. Naturalists who should know say that they sometimes do; Roy Chapman Andrews even was lucky enough to share a woods study with one small singer. I do know that they dance. Dance for sheer joy of living, for sheer delight in quiet moonlight. It couldn't have been for any other reason, because I watched until the dance was done and the dancer went back into his wall to bed, and he was all alone.

It was during raspberry season, a dry one. I went out to check whether the compost piles, back by the berry bushes, needed to have the hose drip on them during the night. I must have moved very quietly because, just as I reached the garden edge, I saw a young wood mouse at the edge of a patch of moonlight, dining luxuriously off a fat raspberry that had fallen conveniently for him.

When he finished, and after he polished whiskers and face-washed like a cat (an odd thing for their two races to have in common, come to think of it), he darted into that moonlit ballroom. And how he danced! Little skips and twirls, a solitary minuet, pirouettes that would have done credit to a prima ballerina.

I tried to breathe as quietly as possible. Because I didn't dare move to look at my watch, I can't say how long my little dancer did his solo. But it must have been ten minutes, at least. He couldn't possibly have been dancing for any reason but joy, and he finished for his own reasons. Nothing scared him. He gave a final whisk, contemplated raspberry bushes for a minute, decided he was full, and went to his wall as unhurriedly as a mouse ever does anything.

Gratefully, I wished him well before I went in to bed, too.

[*27 August 1957*]

First time for this journal since we collected Kay at camp, Sunday. And we're bursting with pride of her: "Best Camper" award for her unit, and her praises simply sung by her nicest counselor. "A joy to have in the unit—wished she'd had her for a full month—etc."

And what pleased me so: "And she's still a child. Not like these pathetic ones, twelve years old with their lipstick and heels."

I've tried to let her grow at her own pace. Not to force her, not to hold her back; it's a delicate balance to hit, and I've probably made more mistakes than I'm aware of. But it's comforting when strangers, unsolicited, say just what you'd like to hear.

She is growing up. That letter she wrote when the ill-advised caramel pulled her new braces out proves it! I've seldom been prouder of anybody. Straight, factual, right to the point—and such a tough letter for a little girl to write.

Tonight, too, she pleased me. Before dinner, energy, after a quiet day, got the better of her and she raced and rolled and somersaulted around the yard like a four-year-old. After dinner, she bathed and dressed in one of her most grown-up dresses to go to an evening showing of *South Pacific* at Rye.

(With a friend, and escorted by friend's father; a very grown up thrill.) Also packed bag to stay with friend overnight, herself, while I brought in laundry. And then, as we waited for the car to call for her, she cocked a humorous eye at me and said: "Mummy, I'm funny right now. Look at me in this dress and these shoes, and my hair fixed, and half an hour ago I was acting younger than Carol." (Who is six, and was then romping with a puppy.) I was so happy; if I can teach her to know herself, and live comfortably with that self, I shall feel that I've discharged well one of the major jobs of a parent.

How much pain and trouble could be avoided, I wonder, if we all knew ourselves better? What we really can—and are likely under a given set of circumstances to—do? What does one teach a daughter?

Be honest; above all, with yourself.

Before you do a big thing, look at the price tag. Add up what the cost will be as well as you can. Then do it or don't do it, depending on whether you think the good results are worth more than the bad will hurt. But above all, look it in the eye—and don't beef once it's done.

Study to learn understanding; it begets itself in return.

Ease into your life so that the shades of gray don't disconcert you too much. (Blacks and whites are so simple—and so seldom encountered!) Keep your eye and hunt your compensations.

And learn to live with yourself. Not within yourself too much, but be quiet and comfortable alone. Lovers cool, people go away or die, jobs get routine, places pall—have the kind of resources that will be there when you need them! There are worse things than loneliness—and many solitary hours need not be lonely at all.

And if you cannot live comfortably, at a reasonable state of peace with yourself, how can you possibly live comfortably with anyone else?

Humor helps. An eye for irony has helped me; a pinch of cynicism, so that minor disappointments don't loom catastrophic.

Interests not tied too closely to people help. If field mouse tracks in snow make your heart lift, if even the roll of a dirty, city pigeon's eye can make you smile, you've got a measure of freedom that will stand by you well. For me, gardens help. At all stages. It's rewarding—and it's work. The kind that wears you out in clean air and makes you sleep at night.

Sometimes I'm sure this quarter-acre is my substitute for the psychiatrist's couch: The heavy work eventually turns your mind off when that mind is chasing fruitlessly in circles, and after it, you sleep. Then you wake to growing things you've helped to grow, and beauty and order that wouldn't be there if you hadn't worked at them. I hate tags, but I suppose "creative outlet" does fairly well to sum up. And all the moments: smell of earth and feel of sun and color of growing things. When things are going well, you can think well as you work with hands more than with brain. When you feel you've got to give, mentally: Go and turn the compost pile!

Perhaps the point of all that is: Pick a job you like within the limitations of the framework of your life. I don't know what I could paint or write (if anything, worth much by high standards); I do know that the concentration time is not presently available. Photography offers a challenge I can't meet because my days do not permit of hours in a darkroom, and my family would be the loser (and thus, I too) if I took to night hours. My life demands sleep to do the job. Having to be here, and in the car and here and there, and loathing housework, gardens seemed to be the answer. (I started them when Kay was three; it's surprising how much you can do in a border and still keep an eye and an ear on a bunch of preschoolers.)

I just used the word "job" advisedly. I wonder where it got its common, slightly unpleasant connotation? A job you love is still a job. Do so few people like the things they do? And if they dislike their vocation, do they simply stultify themselves with television, etc., instead of hunting satisfaction in an avocation? Kill time, instead of live it?

"Job" occurred to me today in the small hours, re marriage.

I can't tell Boo this in so many words, while she's young, but I've got to figure a way to plant the idea somehow, so she can dredge it up when she needs it: Marriage is *not* primarily a great romantic adventure. That's for love affairs. Marriage is a cooperative way of life; a partnership system of doing a job, damn it! A "job" that demands more time and thought and work and adjustment and compromise than most of the things we do in offices or shops or studios, or wherever we earn our livings. The "job" is plain living; the partners decide they'd rather go it together than go it alone, and they've got to manage to grow up enough to learn to cut their losses and give and take to keep going, if it's worth anything. Some people ask too much. (Continued courtship, for example, when the business of living shoves it aside.) Some, as I did, howl to the moon that their individuality has been trampled, when really it's been only slightly chipped around the edges, and they can hold the vital part inviolate and still trot in double harness, if they study to try. And O, at forty and sounding doubtless middle-aged as all get out, I attest to the compensations of the comfortable friendship that can come in when the exciting chase goes out!

[*27 June 1958*]

And now it is darkening and Thrushie has been singing exquisitely outside my window. Bell notes in the maple tree, perfect, round gold globes of sound, breaking at the end into his funny little ascending trill that cracks at the end.

Then he stopped singing to scold something or somebody: furious little yaps. I could see him clearly in my mind, as he (or his forebear) used to sit on the fence behind the playhouse, scolding everything that moved near his nest in the branch that overhung our driveway. He yapped, he spluttered, almost he bounced off his perch while the cinnamon-brown feathers of his small crest rose and fell like a fighting cock's. Such a furious little bird! I did enjoy him, though one worried about his frenzies when the car went in and out, the lawn had to mowed, children played in the little cabin or on the gym set, and cats appeared anywhere on Thrushie's horizon. That absurd bundle of feathered ire could sing like an angel. Evenings without a thrush are incomplete.

(His morning song is too brash and bouyant for me; I'm never *that* awake!)

[*28 June 1958*]

The trouble with really good writing is that so much of it is so quotable the reader gives up taking the time to make notes, or even to digest properly!

Which is unfair of the reader; think of the time and thought the writer took. Reader, do you take time and thought, too, and give the writer his due.

This, because I am reading Virginia Woolf's *Writer's Diary* and find I'd like to make notes for every page. Or else she starts me on a train of thought that winds digressively further and further into sidetrack. . . . . .

The "social reformers and the philanthropists," the politicians and the do-gooders and the busybodies—how they have haunted me these past ten years and how I weary of it! But how to disentangle?

How did I get into it all, anyway? Utter naiveté about community living, for one reason. I couldn't believe for a long time that anybody took most of these causes seriously. I thought they used them partly to fill time in a place that is man-less by day, partly as a springboard to meet new people in the everlasting hope that of a dozen, one may turn out to be the kind you want to spend leisure hours with. When the silly dull crusades were over, I thought, one might find a kindred spirit to turn with toward books and gardens, good talk and the really interesting. But local civic uplift seems to be an end in itself.

Doubtless a worthy end. But O God, it's *not* that important to me. I concede its importance, salute its value, but I'm damned if I can any longer salaam to its practitioners. Too many things supersede it on my personal priority list. For too long, many of them have been neglected.

What do the reformers want? Part of it is honest desire to better things, I concede. But much is a search for the power and the glory, isn't it? The big frog swelling portentously, with self-importance inflating his throat.

There's some of that in all of us, of course. I've wallowed periodically in the sensation of power, God help me! It's exciting to tie into something and feel yourself get it rolling, and I can do it. But the trouble with most of these recent years is that the effort ultimately looked ill-spent to me. Seldom, to the chill pre-dawn eye, has the candle been worth the race.

Later . . .

Why do I dare think about writing, when I find I have almost forgotten how to read? I cannot seem to keep my everlasting self out of any book that provokes thought. Is this evidence of absolute mental degeneration? Or can I explain it, in part at least, by what I read these days: poetry, personal biographies (I mean "personal" in the writing), belles lettres, essays. In short, the introspective. Which provokes me to introspection. An agonizing occupation. Yet a necessary one if I am to survive.

(I almost said: If this family is to survive. Rejected it as presumptuous. But is it? I have a job to do, here. There is pleasure, too, in much of the job. For me. I hope also for HK and K and Beer and the garden. And certainly it would be a different family without me. I think we all prefer it as we are.)

I have been so drilled to shudder at the so-called "egotistical." But must we reject all the ego as we try to subdue it to what we are told is its proper place? When we aren't sure what that place is, we rush so in circles. Fear, or laziness (which one?), making us shy away from self.

But then ego pops out with strange violence over things that are really no important part of self.

What *do* I want (and making at the moment no attempt to assess importance nor arrange in order of priority):

This family well and creatively happy.

A well-ordered house and a well-cared for garden.

The house and garden aforesaid making satisfying setting for us all. (Am I a hog to want a house colored and decorated to please my eye? Red, gray, and brown depress me; blue-green and yellow make my spirit lift. Compromise on white background, then bring the color in. Toni said: "Besides, you look well against white." But when I tried to say to HK that a living room was the setting for the lady of the house, he shouted about egomaniacs. Yet most living rooms are just that.)

Again: I want time to read books and think about them. Books worth thinking about.

And people to talk to about those books and about gardens, and about ideas. Real ideas, not formulae for settling (or un-settling!) political-sociological problems. Damn it, I want to talk to people whose lives and whose business interest me, and talk more about their own ideas and lives and business than they do about how to run other people's!

I want some time and space to myself. First, to try to find myself in, because one way or another I've got pretty thoroughly lost, these ten extroverted years; second, to turn myself to what I consider some accounting, if I can. If I can't, after an honest try, I suppose that will be that and I can always start studying to be madam chairman of something (to me an idiotic goal). . . .

N.B. Maybe the thing is never to get involved in any idea that doesn't interest you? Only move when you're fired with the desire to. Work only for goals that please you.

But then you get to feeling guilty because you aren't pulling your weight in the blasted social group. And you begin to weigh the shades of gray between the black and whites. And, of course, there is value in most of this stuff.

So you flagellate yourself.

[29 *June 1958*]

Sunday. Glorious, blue and gold. Hot sun, gentle wind, smell of new-cut grass, and herbs in the sun. Wonderful when one had begun to think we shouldn't have any summer this year.

Beer lies in shade, enthroned on grass that heightens the color of his eyes. Puff came calling, with sociability and catnip in mind. Somebody has had revels among the clumps, back by the purple cane raspberries; friendly revels, apparently. Not like the time when we found a good four square feet of ground there carpeted with tiger and white cat hair, aftermath of what must have been a major engagement.

Kay appears to present me with a sample of homemade butter and buttermilk. (Since my innards acted up badly yesterday, and we didn't have strawberry shortcake as planned, there was a half-pint of heavy cream with no particular function. And she has always wanted to take eggbeater in hand and see how butter grows. So she has. *Very* fine butter indeed.

(During the war, when I could afford it, I used to buy unrationed cream and roll my own butter, too.)

The catnip reminds me of that major cat fight of our lives here, two springs ago, when the big blue and the Fontecchio's tiger and white had it out in our back, north corner. When I saw who it was I'm afraid I let them go: Fontecchio's tom had been such a trial to us. I hoped he'd lose, or even that they'd do a cats of Kilkenny!

They didn't, and in the end the blue lost and the boss tom became more aggressive than ever. But for at least fifteen minutes neither would give ground; the fence corner limited the battlefield, and they rose, spitting and snarling, in the air, a couple of feet in the air like some fantastic cat-fountain. Afterwards, I found several yards of violets flattened, and the ground carpeted with brown and gray wool.

[1 July 1958]

Remember, about people—anybody: Usually there's very little you can do. Stretch out a hand now and then, hit it right sometimes, but a life is for the guy who's living it to live. You can't swallow it, or be swallowed, or run somebody else's show.

Beware "If I were you—" You're not. And good intentions aren't enough. In some cases they're gratefully received and land on too hard for the learner's good; in others, they're counted intrusion.

[6 July 1958]

I think I'm beginning to get my finger on this damn forty-plus business. And why it hits women harder than men: differently and more shatteringly.

The men are in mid-stride—busy, peak of their powers, and doing.

The women have had ten years or more of intense physical activity and utter mental stagnation, while their children were small.

Then there is the time to think again, and you wonder if you've lost the ability. (You have certainly lost the habit.) And on top of that comes the frightening realization that at least half of active, creative life is gone. ('Til twenty was growth and apprenticeship; after forty is problematical.) It hit me all of a piece: My God! I'm forty-two. That leaves—what? Fifty-two, sixty-two, seventy-two, senility!

This is a sort of inverse adolescence.

Where the adolescent is part exhilarated, part frightened at all the scope of the world spread out before him, where he is trying to grasp it, the middle-aged is beset with a sense of almost insupportable urgency because the perimeter is shrinking. Time *must* be made to count, because time is so terribly limited. These early forties call for personal stocktaking of a most intense order. They're a time of drastic mental upheaval.

It's the mental aspects that are haunting me. The physical aging process definitely is less important. Partly for the reason I told T.: "Of course I mind it less; I have so much less to lose!"

When I was young, I went through ridiculous agonies, wishing to be beautiful. (The female stuff that dreams are made of and duels fought over.) Now I do realize that life is much easier to handle if you're not.

And I look forward to going out of production as a child-bearing animal. I am gladder than I can say that we have Kay. I wish we'd had more. But the time for that's past. Not only because HK and I are past the age where generation would be best for the other, but because I've *got* to see what I can do. Not "do," seen as raising children, as being so terribly interrelated with all the physical aspects of community living, but as individual me for the time I have left . . . .

How can I say "what I want to do" when the immediate need is to disentangle, to disengage, to slough off this maddening bombardment by small particles that had me on the ropes all winter?

And it's hard to disengage when a small voice at the back of my mind keeps driving its needle: But are you sure you're still worth it? What *can* you do? Why didn't you do it before? You haven't written a poem in almost twenty years. Can't blame *that* on anybody else. Try it for size! Try *what*?

Inverse adolescence. More shattering than its earlier form because of the awful urgency. Time running out. (And *what* accomplished?)

All I'm sure of is that I've got to hang onto my nerve and somehow find out if I've lost the ability as well as the habit of creative thought. (But if I have, would it not be better to stay a group animal, endlessly wasting substance on the trifles that make up society's bombardment? Unless you're sure you're worth it, have you the right to say "No"?)

That's one of the serious questions. Still, I think the experiment has to be tried.

P.S. On re-reading: Yes, I used the word "wasting" advisedly. Most "group activity"—committees, conferences, clubs, unions, pressure crowds here and pressure crowds there, getting up petitions—strikes me as a waste. If you can't do it yourself, what is it worth to you as an individual? (Put up or shut up, but for God's sake don't gang up!)

[11 July 1958]

Theater-in-the-round is fast spoiling theater in the conventional for me. It's so much more alive, and you're part of it.

Has anybody ever tried Shakespeare in the round (since his own day)?

What a way to get all those soldiers and crowds and servants and messengers on and off stage. I'd very much like to see it.

[12 July 1958]

Novels should always be written by poets. Style, form, quick movement of the author's mind, description above all. If all novelists can't be poets—and obviously they can't—they should try to serve an apprenticeship at poetry. It would teach them so much about the uses of language: the sharp vignette, the picture etched on crystal, economy with words, counterpoint.

How to call it:
Emotion etched on crystal?
Distilled through rain?
"Emotion" is too strong a word. But a cold word will not do.
"A life in art" sounds sentimental—idiotic.
"Quintessence" is the best word in the language, but it has been overdone.

How to describe wings against water through clear sharp air, when both wings and splash-drops have been schooled by the artist into patterns that reveal so much more than their original form?

Who first said: "Beauty is in the eye of the beholder"?
Or did he say "in"?
There is a vast difference.
"Beauty is the eye of the beholder."
NO!
"Beauty is *in* the eye of the beholder."
You can see the magic is in the "in."

[*13 July 1958*]

Herbs harvested—all we can harbor. Otherwise lazy day. Must get at painting, must get at gardens. Beer says (it's 5:30) that I also must get at his supper. Sun has gone behind the big maple, but a rift in the leaves is permitting one shaft of sunlight to anoint the red beebalm with the color of rubies. Clear, deep bright, unbelievable crimson. Rich beyond belief—and while I wrote this, it faded.

[*25 August 1958*]

Hillier off to conventions. If this weather doesn't clear, he'll be taking a night train instead of a 4 p.m. plane. Gray, fog, overcast, downpour to drizzle. Planes obviously grounded; haven't heard one all day. (Living under domestic approaches to LaGuardia and the Idlewild-Gander route, we know when they are or are not flying.)

Mother, Kay, Beer, and I shall make out nobly (and, as added boon, Frau K is giving the house another of her ineffably thorough cleanings). But *how* I miss HK! Never since I was a small child have I felt so dependent on anyone. And he has been so wonderfully *there*, to depend on. For a woman past forty, and a convalescent at that, I feel idiotically lost. With Monday to Saturday stretching unconscionably long.

Still mentally lazy. Past the stage where mysteries to fill the time effortlessly, and to take one's mind off discomfort, are necessary. But no flights feasible yet. I find I lean to old friends among the authors; return to my literary gods: Benét, Elinor Wylie, Stevenson's letters. . . .

Is there some balance between physical and mental well-being which puts the mental under sedatives when the physical has an unusual job to do? Nature puts the mental in abeyance while the physical gets all the concentration?

I wonder. This has happened to me several times—for shorter periods, immediately following serious illness or operations less severe than this and for the last half of my pregnancy. The body has a big job to do, so the brain rests. What, then, is the converse? I can think only that it is the way one almost forgets the body during periods of intense cerebration.

[*14 September 1958*]

Is there any use trying to write yourself out of a bad mental state when you don't know how you got there or, really, what to put in its place? When you're not sure what you *do want* (that's attainable, at any rate), is there any point in adding up the don't wants? And do's are so nebulous.

Is my chief trouble the fact that they always have been? Did that make me a drifter, or is it the other way around?

T. talks about "being in command of a situation."

I'm trying to remember if ever in my life I have felt that I was. And I can't think of a single occasion. Either some person or group of people drove or cajoled me into doing whatever I did, or else circumstances in general made some course of action expedient, not necessarily the course of action I wanted, or even thought best.

Drifting and making do—expedient, never thought through—forty-odd years of them.

No wonder I bore myself.

And for so long now I've been saying "mine not to reason why" that I wonder if I've lost the ability?

The reason I sold myself on consitutional law, twenty-one years ago, was to try to train my mind to be specific. I am not a specific person. (Prejudiced, yes; analytical, no.)

I did all right with the damn'd law, but none of the training carried over into day-to-day living.

I got out of college with no idea what I wanted to work at; the only thing I was sure of was that I'd rather not work at all! Otherwise, vague ideas of "a job in a publishing house," not that I had (or have) the faintest idea what goes on in publishing houses. But I did, and do, respect books and the people who write them.

So many things people do strike me as things the world could well get on without. But not the creative arts. These we must have.

I got married with a bunch of vague ideas: a permanent love affair with a man I wanted to be with; a foggy concept of, eventually, a way of life involving a big house with lots of land, room for children and animals and lots of guests to bring new ideas in; room enough (I mean land) so we wouldn't even have to think about any people except the ones we liked to think about.

And so car and radio and what-not noises would not be heard unless we made them ourselves.

Social position established firmly enough so no child of mine would ever be forced to be obsessed with proving it as I have been.

"Way of life" including books, animals, outdoors—harmony with nature and freedom from society other than the society of those we wanted.

And, if I must be honest, plenty of "someone elses to do the dirty work."

[*26 January 1959*]

RE CHRISTIANITY:

I've tried, hard and honestly, to buy the religious thing. It would be a great comfort—as well as a weapon against Kay's adopting some undesirable faith later on—but I always stick at the idea that there's a conscious God somewhere, who knows what's going on on this planet. If there is, and He sits up there and does nothing while the innocent suffer, His stewardship seems to me to be deliberately, criminally negligent—or worse. I just can't swallow it.

Some sort of master plan for the universe—that makes sense.

Spiritual potential in man, often unrealized, that should be further developed—quite right.

But if we are His children, why doesn't He do at least half the job parents and teachers do, who do not permit, say, five-year-olds to play with nitroglycerine and switchblade knives?

HK at this point always says, well, probably we're an experiment and God intends us to solve the whole mess ourselves, or else.

It seems logical, but I cannot worship a God like that. I'd as soon worship Khrushchev.

[Undated]

My child finds time hangs heavy on two hands;
If I had six, they'd all be occupied.
Perhaps it all adds up to this:
We learn to catch the minutes and confound the hour.

Because it must, the minute counts for more
Than hours, or even days, when we were young.
Minutes—
    for weeding gardens when there are floors to scrub,
    for touching herbs, for revelling
    in garden smells; for watching the
    catbird who lives in the big syringa,
    for listening to him bubble and bait
    the woodthrush who lives in the small
    maple. Catbird imitations are so
    expert that they can mimic thrush
    family conversation.

I choose the rippling bell note of a thrush
Or catbirds chortling in a lilac bush.

                          When
We reach the busy noontime of our days
Fulfillment is a sum of little things.
I do not worry chiefly for myself,
Men do these things; even their children must
Assume responsibility for what their tribe had done
And pay for guilt, tho' themselves innocent.
Just or unjust, this, as I see it, is.
Only I cannot bear that this good earth
Be torn and wounded past all healing, that
Green growing things may blacken at our touch,
Birds lift their wings against a poisoned sky,
And small wild creatures perish in the fire.

Part Three

KATHERINE L. KRIEGHBAUM, JR.

4. From Kay-K's Notebook

[15 January 1965]

The wind . . .
It howls, fiercely.
It whispers secrets, tenderly.
It rears, savagely.
It caresses, gently.
It fits my moods, perfectly.
It frightens me, because I see my weaknesses through the wind and fear them.
Why must humans be so terribly fallible?
Why must some of us exist in an ethereal state, lacking self-knowledge?
Why must we try, futilely, to plunge blindly on?
Why must we have passions, desires, and enigmas?
Why must we fear material objects when we only have to fear ourselves?
The wind . . .
It howls, fiercely, forever.

[Undated]

With each breath of howling wind, my sorrows, fears, and loneliness are driven further into my heart . . . into my soul. I am like a little child standing on the edge of a ditch, wondering what is on the other side, wondering if I can make it to the other side safely. I know I am evil; I know I am good. I do not know which way the human balance will tip. I have friends; I have had love; I will have love in the future; I have security. And I am still lonely; I am still afraid of the world, and I am still afraid of my own recognized imperfections. And yet, my fears of today will someday be answered, and where will I be then?

[Undated]

I was born in the morn, and I shall die in the night.
With the dawn comes life; warm, gentle, sweet, impulsive, pulsating, tender.
With the dusk comes death; hard, callous, cold.
With the dusk also comes another kind of death; screaming, vicious, painful, frightening to others to witness.
I shall die in this kind of night for my body will want to keep on searching . . . . for a true life.

[27 August 1965]

The full moon sends its pale yet piercing light streaming down upon the forest. Although the light is weak, it discloses many bizarre happenings. The moon is a silent witness to birth, lust, rape, murder, death, and love within the weeds. What man would give to see through these watchful, sleepless eyes!

[*27 August 1965*]

I walk alone, along a dimly-lit path.
I shall always walk alone,
For I am a girl with soul.
I am tormented by trivial things
And by those that do not exist.
I seek solitude and comfort.
I shall continue to search until I find them if I find them.
But now I am alone.
Will I ever gain my self-appointed destiny?

[*2 December 1965*]

This world makes a mockery of everything good, or pure, or
    beautiful . . .
Love is like this . . .
But we are not permitted to love . . .
Or love as we would like to . . .
We must always be worried about time . . .
    How many days, weeks, months have we known each
    other? . . .
    Can we do this now and not be scorned? . . .
    What will happen when we have to part?
We must always be worried about society . . .
    Why won't they let us do that? . . .
    How can they say this is wrong?
We must always worry about what others think . . .
    Why are we too young? . . .
    Can't we feel like this now?
Yet, we could break away . . .
We could damn time, and society, and the others . . .
We could be happy . . .
We could find a place to love in our own way . . .
Tell us where this place is, and we will go there.

[*4 March 1966*]

What was it I was looking for?
A lot of happiness?
A little love?
A little more security?
The flames that guided the search leapt higher . . .
Reaching, crawling towards an unknown goal . . .
An unknown height.
And what did they find . . . this time?
Emptiness . . .
And darkness . . .
Total darkness.

[*23 January 1967*]

Life is spent looking through a rose-colored window, but when you throw that stone of reality at it, attempting to break through, the "rosiness" vanishes.

[*15 March 1967*]

I regret that I have but one life to give to myself. Otherwise, I regret nothing; if I did, I would not have learned what I have, the way I have, and I would have to regret myself, which I could not do because it is the ultimate in hypocrisy, lack of self-respect, and internal (mental) self-damnation and torture. Life is a "good thing"; it is too bad we can't live it more than once, not in retrospect and not reliving it in actuality, knowing what we know now about it and ourselves. Rather, just having the comforting thought of knowing, in certainty, that sometime again, our "souls"* will be in a new person, in a new era, in a different environment, and will have another chance at the wonderful thing called life.

*By "soul", I mean one's innermost thoughts, dreams, hopes, desires, the same communicative ability, goals, ad infinitum, which are tempered and molded to fit into this new social environment so that it wouldn't be archaic, an anachronism, or painfully misfit and avant-garde.

People and Places: A Photographic Album

Japan. August 1960.

Crater Lake, Oregon.

By our brook.

Boulder.

Wagon wheel.

Near Evanston, Illinois. 1968.

"Outlaws." Louisville, Kentucky. 1968.

The Cloisters, New York City.

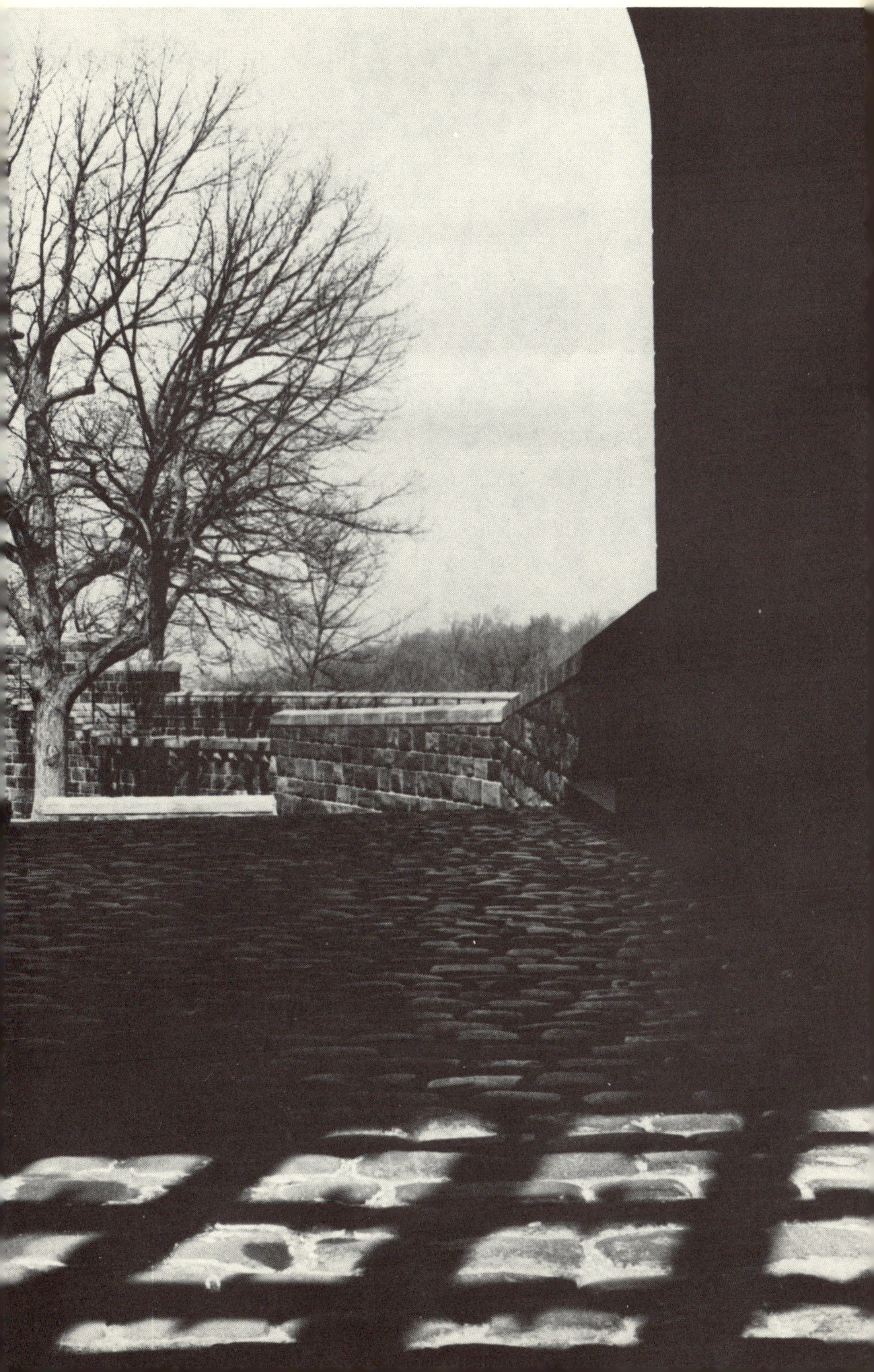

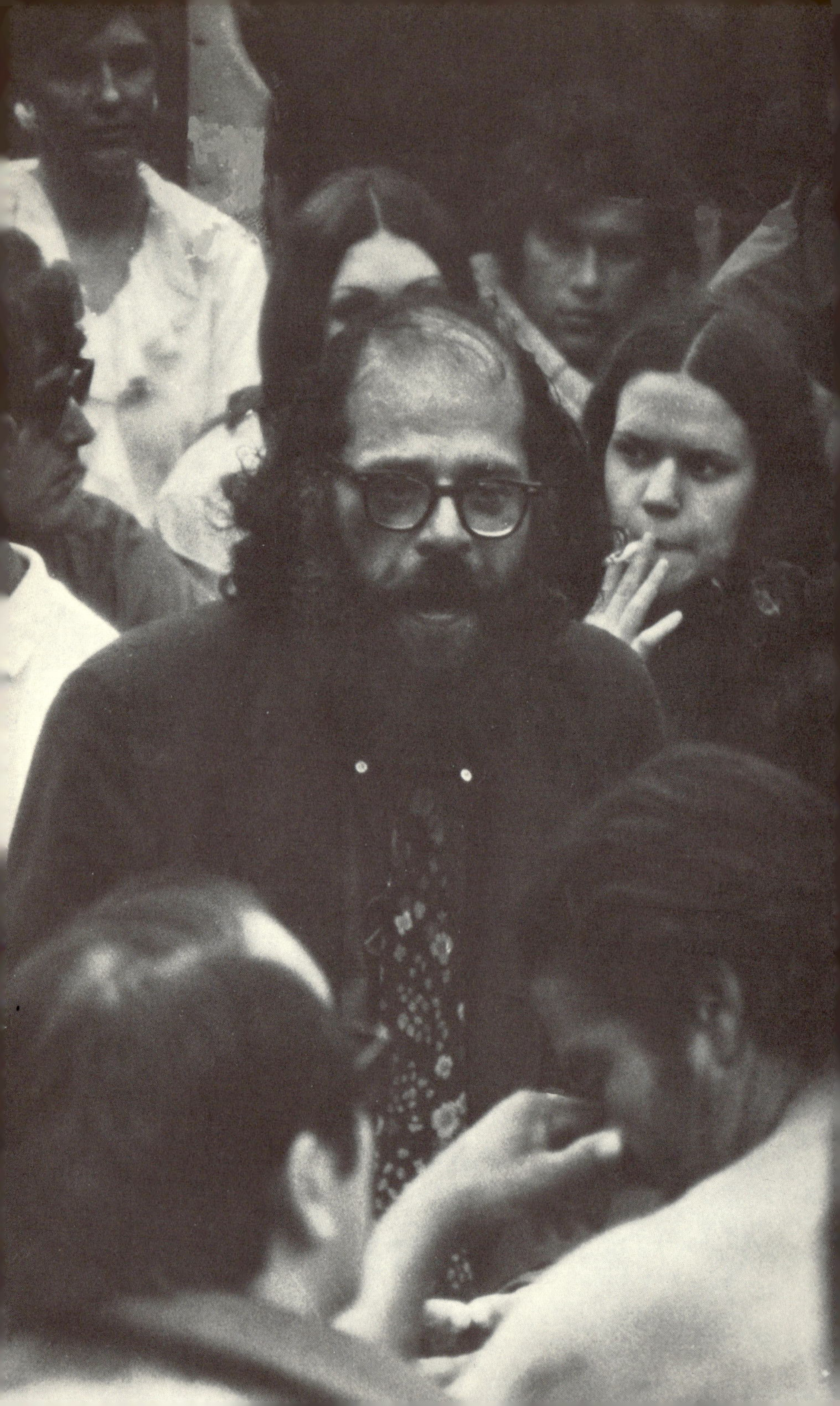

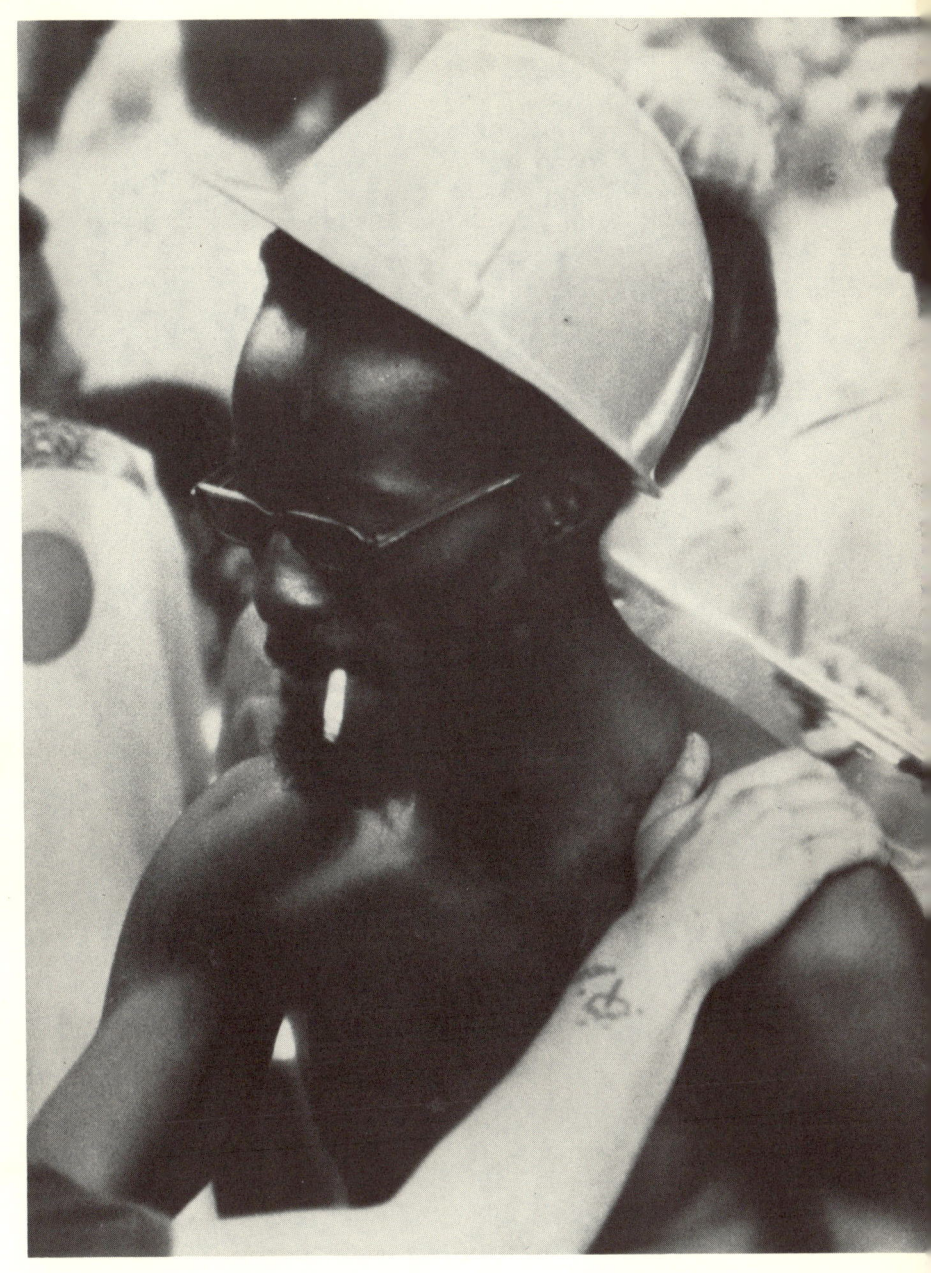

Lincoln Park, Chicago. August 1968.

Allen Ginsberg, Lincoln Park, Chicago. August 1968.

New York University, Washington Square campus.

New York University, Washington Square campus.

Cornell campus. April 1969.

produc... ...spring's ... ...ous ... ...gn.y
insurrection. to recognize and iden..., some of ...
  While condemning the building sei- derlying causes of student disconten...
zure, the trustees criticized the admin- may well fall short of its goal of pro-
istration for being ill prepared to cope moting campus tranquillity.

KAY KRIEGHBAUM—BLACK STAR

MILITANT BLACK STUDENTS DURING CAMPUS INSURRECTION
Lax discipline, poor communication, invisible leadership.

Kay-K's photo in Time, *September 19, 1969.*

Student demonstration, Northwestern University, Evanston, Illinois. Spring 1968.

One of Kay-K's cats in Evanston.

Another feline friend.

Watchful waiters. New York harbor.

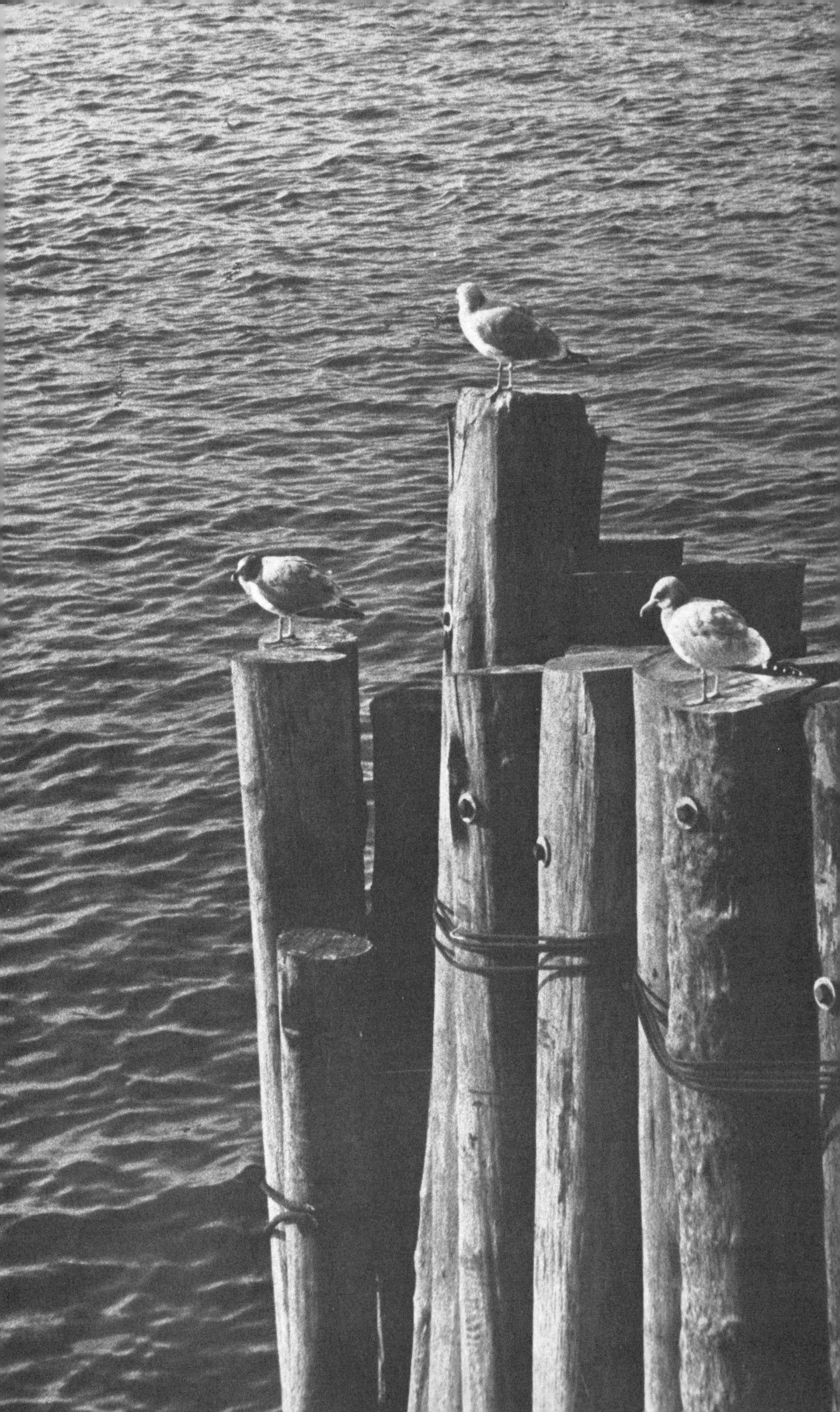

Still water.

Running water.

Curious youth. South Salem, New York.

Handicapped athlete. South Salem, New York.

Winterscape I.

Winterscape II.

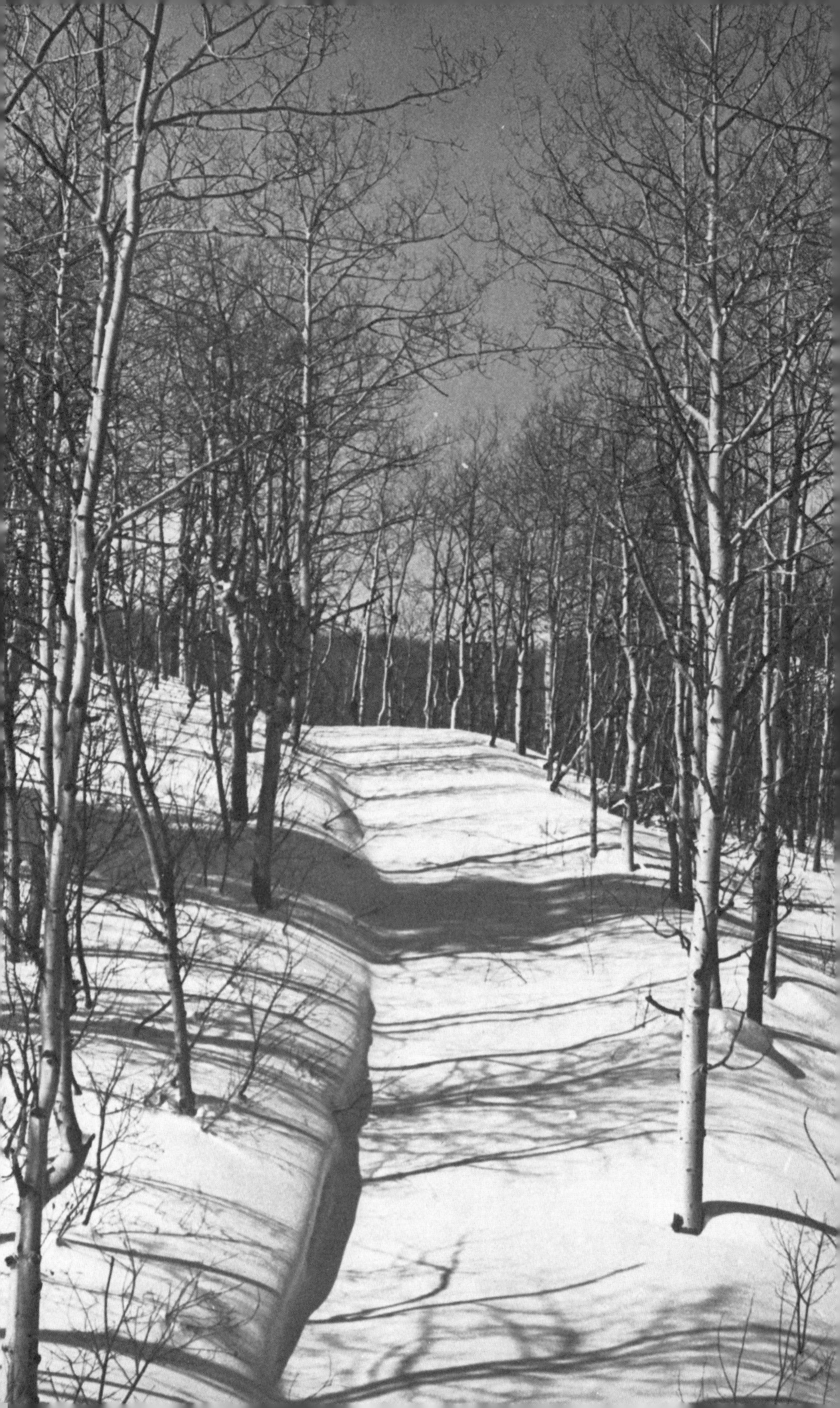

Winterscape IV.

Winterscape III.

Lake George. Summer 1969.

Sunlight on Lake George. Summer 1969.

Lake Michigan shore, near Evanston, Illinois. Winter 1968.

Winter scene, Evanston, Illinois. Winter 1968.

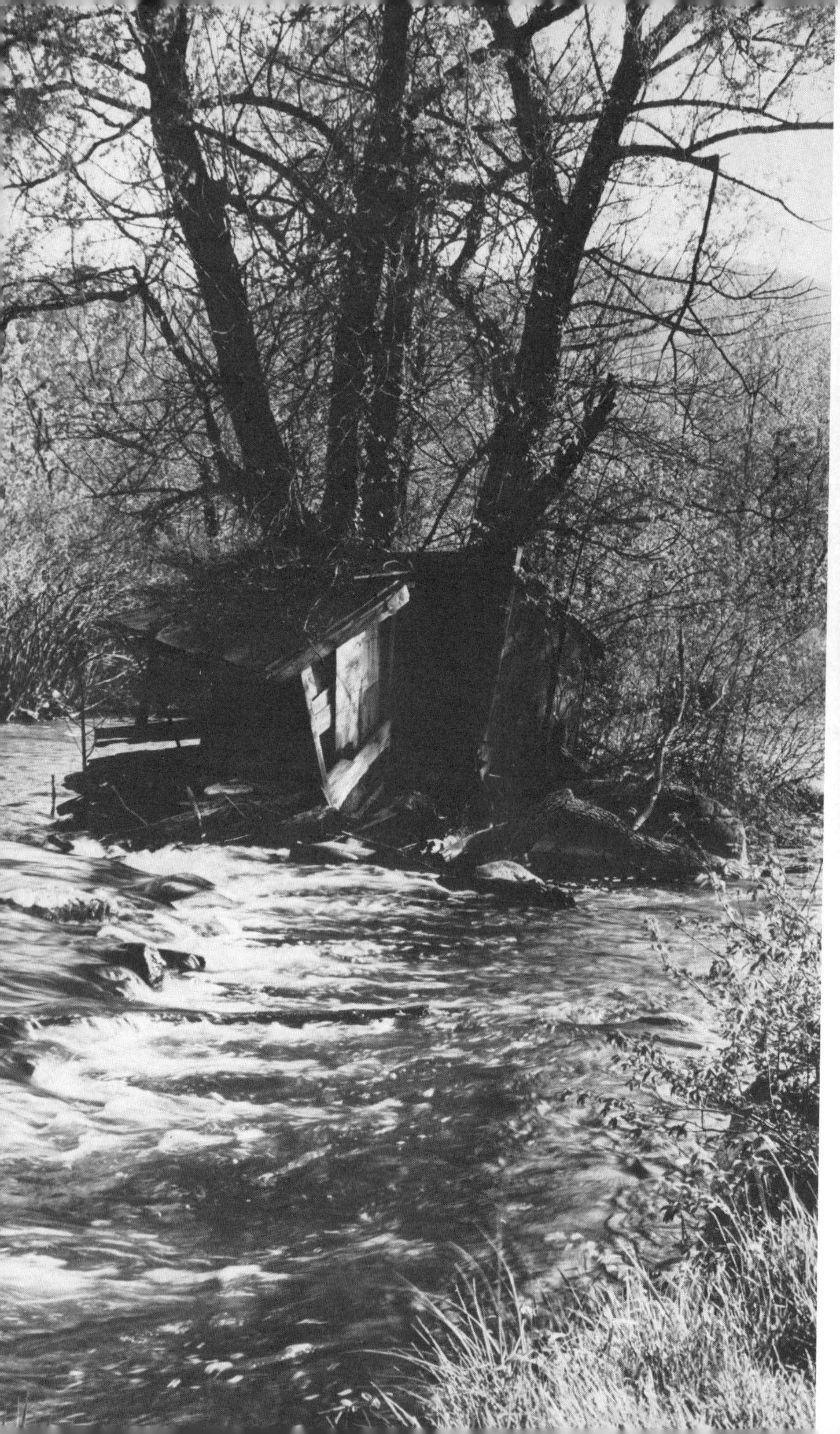

Barn on a hill.

By the stream.

Expo, Montreal. 1968.

Expo, Montreal. 1968.

Abandoned barn.

Neglected cemetery.

Tree Trunk I.

Tree Trunk II.